Defining a Regional Neolithic.
The Evidence from Britain and Ireland

Neolithic Studies Group Seminar Papers 9

Edited by
Kenneth Brophy and Gordon Barclay

Oxbow Books

Published by
Oxbow Books, Oxford, UK

© Oxbow Books and the individual authors, 2009

ISBN 978 1 84217 333 6

A CIP record for this book is available from The British Library

This book is available direct from

Oxbow Books, Oxford, UK
(Phone: 01865-241249; Fax: 01865-794449)

and

The David Brown Book Company
PO Box 511, Oakville, CT06779
(Phone: 860-945-9329; Fax: 860-945-9468)

or

from our website
www.oxbowbooks.com

Cover: *Neolithic timber hall at Claish, Stirlingshire, during excavation in 2001
(© Crown Copyright RCAHMS)*

*Printed in Great Britain by
The Information Press
Eynsham, Oxfordshire*

Foreword

This volume of papers is the ninth set of proceedings from a meeting of the Neolithic Studies Group to be published. As with previous volumes, it includes reflective versions of papers given at a meeting of the group, as well as additional material.

The Neolithic Studies Group is a loose-knit collectivity of archaeologists, mainly from the British Isles and the Atlantic seaboard countries of Europe, with an interest in the Neolithic period. It was formed in the Spring of 1984, the first meeting being held in Cheltenham, Gloucestershire, UK. Since then, the Group has generally met twice a year: Spring and Autumn. The Autumn meetings are held in London and address a specific topical theme. Spring meetings are held outside London to examine at first hand the Neolithic remains of a defined area and consider recent research relevant to the region. Spring field meetings have included: western Ireland, south-east Scotland, eastern Scotland, north Wales, North Yorkshire and Humberside, Northumberland, Wessex, the Channel Islands, Sussex, Cambridge and Grimes Graves, Normandy, Isle of Mann, the Peak District, Caithness, Orkney and Brittany.

All the meetings depend for their success upon the efforts and enthusiasm of local organisers. The occasion of publishing this volume provides an appropriate opportunity to thank all those who have helped organise the Group's meetings in recent years.

Membership of the Neolithic Studies Group is open to anyone active in studying any aspect of the Neolithic period in Europe. The present membership list, which stands at around 250 individuals, includes: academic staff, researchers and students from universities and colleges in several European countries; museum curators and museum-based research and field staff; and field archaeologists from national and local government organisations and from archaeological trusts and units. There is no application procedure or subscription fee to join the Group; members are simply those currently on the mailing list. Anyone can ask to be added to the mailing list at any time, the only rule of the Group is that names are deleted from the list if the individual concerned misses four meetings in a row (ie. two years) and has not contacted the Group Co-ordinators asking to be kept on the list during that time.

For further information about the history of the Group, details of forthcoming events and publications, and details of how to join our mailing list, visit the Group's web site:

www.neolithic.org.uk

As already mentioned, the Group relies on its members to organise meetings so that this responsibility is shared round. There are two Co-ordinators who look after the mailing list and finances, and who juggle offers to arrange meetings so that there is a fair spread of venues and themes.

We hope that you will find this volume of papers published by the Neolithic Studies Group useful, and we look forward to seeing you at one of our future meetings.

Timothy Darvill and Kenneth Brophy
(Neolithic Studies Group Co-ordinators)

Contents

This volume of papers represents the rather belated proceedings of the meeting of the Neolithic Studies Group held in Burlington House, Society of Antiquaries of London, on 12 November 2001 (most of the papers were submitted in near final form in 2002). The topic of that particular meeting of the group, 'Regional diversity in the Neolithic of Britain and Ireland', drew a wide range of papers, the majority of which are represented in this volume; an additional paper (Chapter 3) was offered and accepted after the meeting. The session itself was organised by the editors of this volume. Although the day meeting itself was not organised along any thematic lines, a loose tripartite structure has been applied: *Defining regional Neolithics*; *Material culture*; and *Regional and local studies*.

The day meeting itself was driven by a series of four questions, and by way of introduction to the volume, Barclay has expanded on these, and his introductory comments made on the day, to form a comprehensive introduction to this volume (Chapter 1). This is followed by a more abstract contribution from Brophy (Chapter 2), analysing that most familiar of tools for the display of archaeological data, the distribution map. These two papers set out some of the parameters for the volume, essentially *Defining regional Neolithics* for the reader.

The two papers that follow address the role *Material culture* plays in both defining and characterising regional trends, covering a diverse range of forms of material culture, starting with an analysis of querns by Roe (Chapter 3). Loveday (Chapter 4) considers a wider range of objects from the Neolithic of Yorkshire and beyond. Artefacts in much earlier archaeological studies were used, through typology and culture-history, to establish misguided models of Neolithic traditions in the British Isles, but these three studies aim to re-think artefacts within a different theoretical framework.

The third section of the book considers a series of *Regional and local studies*, the definition of both 'regional' and 'local' being ambiguous at best here, suggesting, as do the contributions, that a number of cross-cutting scales of identity were in operation in the Neolithic. Papers focus largely on the so-called Irish Sea Zone: Cummings (Chapter 5) focuses on north-west Wales and south-west Scotland; Watson and Bradley, and Clare (Chapters 6–7) on Cumbria; and Cooney on a series of islands off the Irish coast (Chapter 9). Ireland is considered in more detail by Carleton Jones (Chapter 10), while a diversion from the West Coast is provided by Clay (Chapter 8) in a detailed analysis of a large body of Neolithic data from the East Midlands.

One of the defining characteristics of the day meeting, and this volume, was that contributors steered clear of the 'usual suspects' – Wessex and Orkney. This is not to say that the volume contains a number of rival regions, nor indeed that individual contributors are describing clear-cut Neolithic regions. However it does suggest, along with notable historiographies of the Neolithic (*e.g.* Barclay 2001), that there is something in the air that demands a closer inspection of the evidence elsewhere. Not only that, but interpretations should be applied that have an element of local contingency rather than drawing on universal theories applied in the old 'core' areas in the south and far north of the Britain. The papers here represent for us an embodiment of the sentiment so admirably expressed over a decade ago by Harding (1991), who described Wessex as unique, not typical.

The editors would like to thank the Society of Antiquaries of London, especially Dai Morgan Evans, for organising the use of the Society's rooms in Burlington House, and for coping with a full house on the day. Our thanks also to the contributors on that day back in 2001, and for all those who offered a paper for this volume: your patience has been noted and appreciated.

The whole concept of a 'regional Neolithic' is one that has a various potential interpretations, and we hope that this volume as a whole presents papers that grasp with this problematic but hugely exciting area of Neolithic studies.

Barclay, G. J., 2001, 'Metropolitan' and 'Parochial'/'Core' and 'Periphery': a historiography of the Neolithic of Scotland. *Proceedings of the Prehistoric Society*, 67, 1–16.

Barclay, G. J. and Russell-White, C. J., 1993, Excavations in the ceremonial complex of the fourth to second millennium BC at Balfarg and Balbirnie, Glenrothes, Fife. *Proceedings of the Society of Antiquaries of Scotland*, 123, 43–110.

Harding, J., 1991, Using the unique as the typical: monuments and the ritual landscape. In P. Garwood, D. Jennings, R. Skeates and J. Toms (eds), *Sacred and Profane. Proceedings of a Conference on Archaeology, Ritual and Religion*. Oxford. Oxbow. 141–151.

Gordon Barclay and Kenny Brophy
May 2007

List of Contributors

GORDON BARCLAY
Historic Scotland
Longmore House
Salisbury Place
Edinburgh EH9 1SH

RICHARD BRADLEY
Department of Archaeology
University of Reading
Whiteknights
PO Box 227
Reading RG6 6AB

KENNETH BROPHY
Department of Archaeology
Gregory Building
University of Glasgow
Glasgow G12 8QQ

TOM CLARE
Biological and Earth Sciences
   Division
Liverpool John Moores University
James Parson Building
Byrom Street
Liverpool L3 3AF

PATRICK CLAY
ULAS
School of Archaeology and Ancient
   History
University of Leicester
Leicester LE1 7RH

GABRIEL COONEY
Archaeology Department
National University College Dublin
John Henry Newman Building
Belfield
Dublin 4
Ireland

VICKI CUMMINGS
School of Forensics and Investigative
   Sciences
University of Central Lancashire
Preston
Lancashire PR1 2HE

CARLETON JONES
Department of Archaeology
National University of Ireland
Galway
University Road
Galway
Ireland

ROY LOVEDAY
10 New Avenue
Rearsby
Leicestershire LE7 4YU

FIONA ROE
Blackthorn Cottage
Vicarage Lane
Hillesley
Wotton-under-Edge
Gloucestershire GL12 7RA

AARON WATSON
PO Box 726
Lancaster LA1 1XS

Chapter 1

Introduction:
a regional agenda?

Gordon Barclay

In suggesting the agenda for the day meeting Kenneth Brophy and I posed four questions to the speakers:

1. In what way is, and in what areas are, inter-regional contrast or variation manifested?

2. Can boundaries be recognized and if they can, are they short-lived or persistent?

3. Are some areas (*e.g.* Orkney or the Boyne Valley) of particular, trans-regional significance, or are such perceptions a product of modern concerns?

4. Can material culture be seen as a reflection of actual regional variation in the Neolithic, and if so, what role does it play in creating and sustaining identities?

The reader must decide how successfully we, and the contributors, were.

It was as recently as 1985 that Ian Kinnes pointed out that 'There is no reason, other than that of modern political expediency, why the "Scottish Neolithic" should exist as an entity' (1985, 16). He might as well have written the 'British Neolithic'. Childe, (1935, 1) wrote that '...Scotland is not an arbitrary political division but possesses...a personality of her own'. This is not an accurate assessment, and the considerable variation in the landscape, accessibility and carrying capacity of the regions of Scotland, mean that the origin and development of human settlement will inevitably have been varied. More recently Gabriel Cooney (2000) had still to make the same argument for Ireland – that there was no homogeneous Irish Neolithic. In parts of England outside the 'archetypal English landscape' of the south and south-west (Barclay 2001, 2004), Frodsham, Harding and others have shown that this problem affects other parts of England in the same way as in the surrounding countries (Harding *et al.* 1996).

Kinnes' 1985 statement seems now a statement of the blindingly obvious – two decades ago it did not. Until the 1970s or 1980s the assumption, conscious or unconscious, was that there was a relatively unified British Neolithic; as Harding (1997) has commented, an approach that recognizes regionality but consigns it to a minor role in narratives, has had a dominant place in the literature. The 'unified Neolithic' model had four main origins:

1. archaeology had been working with limited amounts of reliable data from survey and excavation;

2. a large proportion of that data was from a limited number of areas that had seen concentrations of activity by archaeologists or in the antiquarian period. The development of explanatory models inevitably relied heavily on these data sets;

3. some of the 'core' areas of study were lacking certain sorts of data (particularly for settlement). In combination with the overall thinness of data, the creation of coherent narratives necessitated the drawing together of data that now seems to have more complicated relationships, and a better understood local context;

4. the data for the 'core' areas was given a primacy over data from other areas – it was the norm against which other material was seen to vary; that assignment of primacy, and the concentration of archaeological effort in those areas in the first place, may reflect deeper-seated concerns within the archetypal English landscape (*cf.* Barclay 2004).

The archaeological result of the 'unified' model was a generalized prehistory that overemphasized similarity, underplayed diversity and assigned a primacy to data and explanation in 'core' areas. This is a characteristic shared with written British history, but that discipline has for longer been conscious of the historical and cultural effects on the writing of history within Britain. 'Four Nations' history – supposedly history of the constituent parts of the United Kingdom – is largely a history of England, erected as a sort of 'norm', with inconsistent inclusion of references to material or events in other parts of the country. Pittock (1999, 98) characterizes it as history '…which seeks conformity and minimizes differences and nuances'. These descriptions are unfortunately true of many recent accounts of British prehistory (*e.g.* Longworth and Cherry 1986; Dyer 1990; Parker-Pearson 1993; Schama 2000).

The historiography of the Neolithic is a study in itself – and there can be no 'final' account. I have written one, relevant to my own area of study (Barclay 2001) and others need to be written for other parts of Britain and Ireland.

A consistent element in the argument for regional perspectives for the Neolithic of Ireland and Scotland is the suggestion that models erected in one area on relatively well-studied data-sets have been used uncritically to explain data in other areas. As we learn more about the Neolithic the use of broad-brush explanations becomes less sustainable. We cannot ignore the very clear evidence for inter-regional contact, such as the wide distribution of stone axes, types of pottery and burial and ceremonial practice (as represented by pottery and monument types); however, it has been strongly argued that material must be placed in its regional context before broader parallels are sought or a 'national' picture drawn.

As more data – better survey, aerial photography and particularly the results of excavation – have become available for non-core areas, the homogenizing models have been found wanting to explain increasingly varied data. The issue rose to the top of the agenda from the early 1990s with, on the one side, the promotion of the mobile Neolithic hypothesis beyond its natural home in southern England, and on the other, criticism by workers in northern England, Ireland and Scotland.

Of the four questions asked at the start of this introduction, the individual's answer to the third, *'Are some areas (e.g. Orkney or the Boyne Valley) of particular, trans-regional significance, or are such perceptions a product of modern concerns?'*, perhaps reveals one's view of the extent to which the origins and development of the Neolithic of these islands is regionally determined, or whether one is still committed to a sort of 'core/periphery' model. That there are still lines drawn between two camps was brought home to me when one of the anonymous referees for my 'historiography' (Barclay 2001) paper noted that a criticism of it 'would be the default assumption throughout that all areas are equal, just different; that because Orkney is not Wessex, it cannot be a phenomenon of the same kind…Yorkshire may indeed be another "bright spot" between Stonehenge and Brodgar, but that does not diminish the luminosity of the other two'. This – perceptions of importance – was one of the themes Kenneth Brophy and I wanted to explore in the day meeting; to what extent are areas like Wessex, the Boyne Valley, and Orkney 'centres' in prehistory, or merely 'central' to the thinking of a majority of prehistorians? The survival of impressive monuments and the resultant prolonged attention has resulted in the latter, but not demonstrated the former. Were these 'luminous' centres of particular importance in the past, or is their modern status a reflection of the concerns of prehistorians during the last century or so? We have seen Wessex and Orkney suggested as places of pilgrimage – but are the pilgrims only modern prehistorians? Let us consider for a moment some complexes of monuments that have come to light more recently. How would our perceptions of relative importance be affected if the complexes at Dunragit (Thomas 2001, 138–40, 2004) or Hindwell (Gibson 1996) were not of perishable timber, but had survived in stone to the 19th century or beyond?

This is the nub – do we start with an assumption that certain areas are 'primary' or do we have to test and demonstrate such assumptions? In approaching this issue we have to overcome decades of archaeological discourse, as well as the deeper cultural influences on the writing of history that I have set out elsewhere (Barclay 2001). However, we must be careful not to replace 'national' prehistories with micro-regional approaches that underplay the very real shared traditions, and complex relationships between regions, between Britain and Ireland, and between the British Isles and mainland Europe.

In 1996, in the publication of the Neolithic Studies Group meeting on houses, Thomas (1996, 6) suggested that we 'should think of the European Neolithic less as a unified and homogenous entity and more as a series of historical developments which are only loosely connected with each other'. This seems a useful place to start in considering the Neolithic of these islands. Clearly there are strong relationships and shared traditions, but we can see that differences are greater than used to be thought. We must explore the characteristics that suggest shared origins and traditions – for example long mounds, timber mortuary structures within them, plain round-bottomed pottery, the widespread distribution of henges – as well as those that suggest quite different approaches – the apparent absence of interrupted-ditch enclosures north of central Scotland, the vigorous early Neolithic round barrow traditions of Perthshire and Yorkshire, and regionally-constrained distributions of types of artefacts and monuments.

We are in the early stages of the exploration, but we believe the meeting, the proceedings of which form the basis of this volume, was a useful contribution to this important area of study.

Bibliography

Barclay, G. J., 2001, 'Metropolitan' and 'Parochial'/'Core' and 'Periphery': a historiography of the Neolithic of Scotland. *Proceedings of the Prehistoric Society*, 67, 1–16.

Barclay, G. J., 2004, 'Four nations prehistory': cores and archetypes in the writing of prehistory. In R. Philips and H. Brocklehurst (eds), *History, nationhood and the question of Britain*. Basingstoke. Palgrave. 151–159.

Childe, V. G., 1935, *The Prehistory of Scotland*. London. Kegan Paul, Trench and Trubner.

Cooney, G., 2000, *Landscapes of Neolithic Ireland*. London. Routledge.

Dyer, J., 1990, *Ancient Britain*. London. Batsford.

Gibson, A., 1996, A Neolithic enclosure at Hindwell, Radnorshire, Powys. *Oxford Journal of Archaeology*, 15.3, 341–348.

Harding, J., 1997, Interpreting the Neolithic: the monuments of North Yorkshire, *Oxford Journal of Archaeology*, 16.3, 279–295.

Harding, J., Frodsham, P. and Durden, T., 1996, Towards an agenda for Neolithic Studies in Northern England. In P. Frodsham (ed.), *Neolithic Studies in No-man's Land* (Northern Archaeology 13/14). Newcastle: Northern Archaeology Group. 189–201.

Kinnes, I., 1985, Circumstance not context: the Neolithic of Scotland as seen from the outside. *Proceedings of the Society of Antiquaries of Scotland*, 115, 15–57.

Longworth, I. and Cherry, J., 1986, *Archaeology in Britain since 1945*. London. British Museum Press.

Parker Pearson, M., 1993, *Bronze Age Britain*. London. Batsford/English Heritage.

Pittock, M., 1999, *Celtic Identity and the British Image*. Manchester. Manchester University Press.

Schama, S., 2000, *History of Britain volume 1. At the edge of the world 3000BC–1603AD*. London. BBC.

Thomas, J., 1996, Neolithic houses in mainland Britain and Ireland – a sceptical view. In T. Darvill and J. Thomas (eds), *Neolithic Houses in Northwest Europe and Beyond* (Neolithic Studies Group Seminar Papers 1). Oxford. Oxbow. 1–12.

Thomas, J., 2001, Neolithic enclosures: reflections on excavations in Wales and Scotland. In T. Darvill and J. Thomas (eds), *Neolithic enclosures in Atlantic Northwest Europe* (Neolithic Studies Group Seminar Papers 6). Oxford. Oxbow. 132–143.

Thomas, J., 2004, The ritual universe. In G. J. Barclay and I. A. G. Shepherd (eds), *Scotland in Ancient Europe. The Neolithic and Early Bronze Age of Scotland in their European context*. Edinburgh. Society of Antiquaries of Scotland. 171–8.

Chapter 2

The map trap: the depiction of regional geographies of the Neolithic

Kenneth Brophy

'A good map tells a multitude of little white lies; it suppresses truth to help the user see what needs to be seen'

(Monmonier 1996, 25)

INTRODUCTION

There is compelling evidence and a sound theoretical basis for supposing that there were regional traditions of society, of material culture, and of identity within the Neolithic of the British Isles (*cf.* Bradley 1984; Sharples 1992; Thomas 1998; Cooney 2000; Barclay 2001). One of the most effective ways of communicating the idea of regional traditions is through the use of distribution maps, a time-honoured tool of archaeological discourse for well over a century. In this paper, I will argue that distribution maps are problematic for a number of reasons. Firstly, that (obviously) they are a peculiarly modern and detached way of depicting spatial relationships that say more about the way that we organise data than any past reality. Secondly, that they are generally produced without much reflection on the mechanics and language of map-making. Finally, I suspect that the true power of maps as a persuasive tool of communication is not readily appreciated.

In (re)constructing past meaningful networks of material culture we risk falling between two extremes. On one hand there is the locational and grid referenced point in the landscape (the 'site' or 'findspot') typical of so many distribution maps, and on the other, the generalised overview (the 'region' or even the distribution map itself). This leaves a gap, a gap that Tilley (1994, 3) suggests is rarely successfully bridged. This is a gap that runs between the individual and the communal, one that not so much needs bridged but rather acknowledged as a subtle network of complex relationships of significance. As Ingold (2000) argues, the way that we visualise movement within the space that we inhabit is neither as a causal chain of grid references nor a top-down vertical overview, but rather a perspective rooted in inhabitation, memory, experience and emotion. So here I would like to offer a critical reflection of the way that archaeologists usually graphically depict regions in the Neolithic – through traditional mapping – because the way that we map is different from the way that we engage with, and account for our world.

But more than this, maps are not merely presentational devices. Rather they have a language and context all of their own, a heritage that has left them unquestionable and trustworthy – when in fact this familiarity only screens us from complex decision-making processes that took place in the actual construction of the map itself (Monmonier 1996). My argument is that through distribution maps we are implicitly saying something significant about the way that the past was organised over wide geographical areas projected from a finite number of fixed points within this area, translating point to space data in one all-too-easy step. We are all familiar with images of regional Neolithics, usually dots or symbols on a background map, with titles and legends, and the symbology used and data included. So this paper is concerned with how we visualise the regional Neolithics discussed in more detail in the rest of this volume.

THE STATUS OF DISTRIBUTION MAPS

> *'Lurking beneath the distribution of the dots on the map was a spatial process and a causality to be discovered'*
>
> (Tilley 1994, 9)

The unquestioning use of distribution, or chloropleth, maps in archaeology has survived the buffeting of various theoretical waves over the decades. They are iconic tools for displaying archaeological data and we would hardly expect an overview of some aspect of the Neolithic not to include at least one. It is a technique of depiction and persuasion in general Neolithic volumes and papers written throughout the twentieth century and beyond, from Childe (1947, throughout) to Piggott (1954, 131 and 291) to Thomas (1999, 19, 20, 130 and so on). (Although it was still possible to offer syntheses of classes of monuments without recourse to such maps in the 1930s, such as Curwen (1930) and Piggott (1939). Earlier syntheses depended more heavily on artefact drawings and rudimentary site plans (*e.g.* Anderson 1886).)

Distribution maps are part of the common currency of archaeological discourse. They have a vocabulary, a language of their own, which is familiar and understandable to us, as archaeologists. For instance, elements of the maps are regarded as a given, and need no mention in the key – from the coastline (usually depicted in unnecessarily spurious detail) and sea surface, to arrows requiring no N to show that they are pointing northwards. There is a shared understanding between creator and reader that allows us to read and recognise the meaning of the map. Whatever their actual purpose, distribution maps in archaeology are, if read uncritically (as they usually are) seen as immutable and beyond question, with the sometimes explicit, usually implicit, warning that they depict only our current state of knowledge and discoveries and as such are a white wall onto which we project our archaeological knowledge. These distributions are based on typologies and classifications – without these, we could not begin to construct our regional archaeologies (Brophy 2005).

Reading maps is not a simple process. There is more to a map that knowing how to work out grid references or understanding the nature of contours. We learn these difficult spatial and visualization skills – the translation of an abstract figure (grid reference) to place; 3D visualization and so on – at school (*cf.* Harrison and Harrison 1988; Kemp 1989). There, we also learn how to use maps, reading them, and working with them. Only by understanding the whole and learning the rules or grammar of the map can we have understanding (or rather, a basis for interpretation). The map is a tool. Maps can also become arbiters of authority, both of the government-run Ordnance Survey, and of the cartographer. In this respect they appear to be an unquestionable, objective and utterly reliable data source.

But we should not be lulled into a cosy relationship with maps. Maps are oxymoronical, simultaneously depicting objectively the spatial relationship of the data, while at the same time asserting and proving the same relationships. Maps are mere devices, subjective documents that should be read interpretively, but appear to us as objective depictions of some external reality albeit abstractly depicted (Wood 1993; Monmonier 1996). This contradiction allows the depiction of the results of archaeological enquiry to become a persuasive version of the past. It is precisely because we view distribution maps as reliable and inherently meaningful that they can be weak and biased methods of depicting patterns in the past.

As many archaeologists have shown in recent decades, our subjective role in generating interpretations of the past is all too often ignored (*cf.* Shanks and Tilley 1987; Bender 1998, 78–86; Hodder 1999, 102–104). We should understand that maps are not neutral conveyors of data, any more than excavation and survey results are objectively derived (Lucas 2001; Hodder 1997). Maps are subjective and ambiguous, but this is rarely acknowledged.

> *'And this, essentially, is what maps give us, reality, a reality that exceeds our vision, our reach, the span of our days, a reality we achieve in no other way. We are always mapping the invisible or the unattainable or the erasable, the future or the past .... And through the gift the map gives us, transmuting it into everything it is not ... into the real'*
>
> (Wood 1993, 4–5).

PROBLEMATIC ELEMENTS OF DISTRIBUTION MAPS

> *'They [distribution maps] have anatomies'*
>
> (Wood 1993, 138)

Distribution maps are read and interpreted in their own right as a whole consisting of a seamless blend of layers, from background topography to foreground archaeological data. Yet the apparent authority of maps is despite their abstract symbolism, the incomplete data, and often their banality. Beneath the surface of every distribution map, there are a range of visual and intellectual cues that come together to make the map comprehensible. It is only by thinking about the conventions that both restrict and govern their production that we can begin critically to assess how they impact on us, the reader.

Maps are the product of a whole series of decisions; the choice to make the map, the choice of symbols used, the choice of data to include and exclude, the scale (in time and space), the location of the boundaries, the legend, the orientation, the title and finally the caption beneath the map at the bottom of the page (Wood 1993). Most conform to geographical or archaeological standards that it is assumed the reader will understand, accept and even expect. Some of these decisions shape the way that the chosen data is presented, and choices will change meaning. Some of these choices will inevitably influence the way that the data will be interpreted, and not always in a way that the creator of the map intended.

In this the main part of this paper I want to look at some examples of archaeological distribution maps to illustrate the main building blocks of mapmaking and how they can augment or subvert the intentions of the mapmaker. These distribution maps have not been selected for any other reason than illustrative purposes; they are representative of a host of similar maps that are familiar to all archaeologists. Importantly, I want to stress that the corollary of my earlier contention that archaeologists do not always appreciate the power or language of maps is that these maps were not designed with the intention to mislead the 'reader'. Rather I want to show that our (subconscious) understanding of maps, and the data encoded within them, is far more sophisticated than the conscious production of maps; therefore, the use of symbols, boundaries, data and scales is far more significant than we think. This paper is not a critique of mapmakers, but instead is an attempt to encourage innovative and reflective use of maps in archaeology through a better understanding of the language of maps. Reflection should focus on the reason for the production of the map as well as its design.

SYMBOLS

> *'Next came the biggest display – a projection of Russia and its surrounding territory and sea. Here would be shown the projected tracks of SAC bombers as they headed towards their assigned targets. The targets could also be shown. Primary targets were represented by triangles, and secondary targets by squares. These targets were mostly missile and bomber bases, with a few radar positions and defensive missile complexes. Some were near big centers of population, some were not. But it was impossible to tell from the display. Centers of population were not shown'*
>
> (Southern 1997, 29–30).

The choice of symbols used in distribution maps is both significant and telling. A semiotics of mapmaking is possible, reminding us that symbols are merely signifiers, ink marks on a page that depict something other than themselves (an object, a monument, a site) and all the associations that go with the signified. Mapmakers can employ a number of different symbologies known either as plan information or plan free information (Wood 1993). These can range from abstract geometrical symbols with a fixed grid reference, to a shape symbol sized to a quantitative scale (again spatially situated), to abstract symbols or shapes that represent what is being depicted but not to scale. The latter are often used to indicate patterns rather than exact spatial location. When deciding on symbols, variations in size, shape, colour/hue, texture and orientation have to be considered (Monmonier 1996, 19–20). Symbology can also include zones or blocks of shading with solid or ambiguous boundaries (see below).

Each symbol we see on a distribution map has to have been selected, for the spatial data that has to be conveyed, but also in some cases for the visual imagery of the symbol, even symbol as metaphor/simile. The choice of symbology can be used to indicate patterns of relative distribution. Figure 2.1 (from Ashmore 1996, 57) depicts a fine example of this, with the chambered tombs of Scotland represented by stylised drawings of chambered tomb 'types'. Each symbol represents many tombs, not one, and there is no mathematical

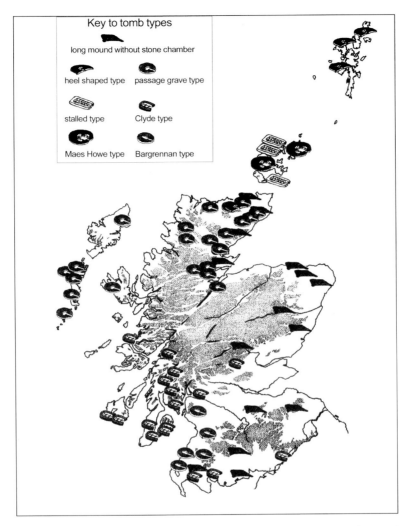

Figure 2.1 The use of symbols 1: passage graves in Scotland, 4000–2500BC (from Ashmore 1996, 57).

equivalence to this, that is, the symbols have no specific numeric or spatial value in themselves. Nor do they represent chronological constancy – rather these tomb types span over two millennia of Scotland's prehistory. This distribution map is generally making the point firstly that there are lots of different types of passage graves across Scotland; and, second, that they exist in discrete regional groupings.

More traditionally, we are used to seeing abstract geometric symbols, with each of those symbols representing one unit in that particular location. Of course, this apparently neutral

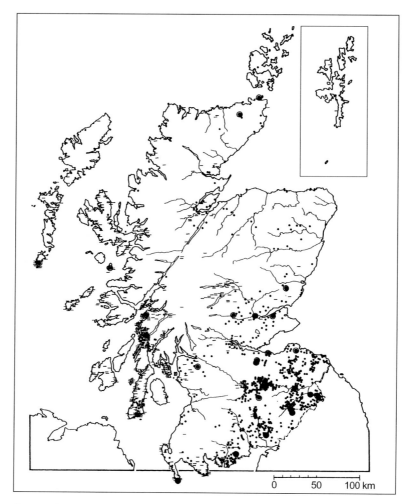

Figure 2.2 The use of symbols 2: distribution of Scottish hillforts and duns (from Armit and Finlayson 2003, 181, fig 10.5).

schema can be subverted. Perec (1997, 190) has observed that apparently neutral symbols – for instance the letters of the alphabet – are loaded with hidden social values. For example, A is regarded as being superior to B in certain contexts such as essay grades. In the same way, the choice of abstract symbols can give a layer of additional, implicit, meaning beyond a neutral spread of data. Moving briefly outwith the Neolithic, we can see in Figure 2.2 an example of how the reader could subvert apparently abstract symbolism in a distribution map showing certain Iron Age settlement sites in Scotland (from Armit and Ralston 2003, 181). Here a short horizontal line represents a dun, a black dot equals a small hillfort, and a dot inside a larger circle represents a hillfort with an internal area greater than 2.5ha. These

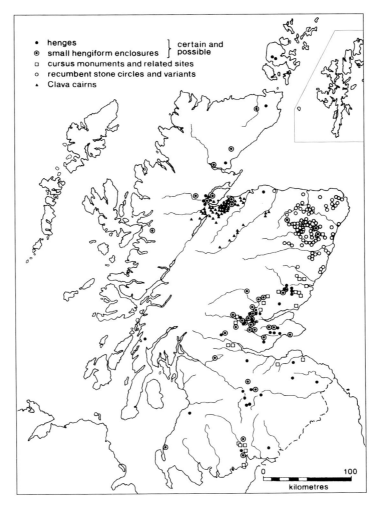

Figure 2.3 The use of symbols 3: map showing distribution of various Neolithic and Bronze Age monuments in Scotland (from Barclay 2003, 136, fig 8.2).

symbols = 1 site, and have spatial accuracy. The chosen symbols also suggest to the reader (or the reader reads this into the map) the idea of core and periphery. The larger hillfort symbol dominates and gives the impression of a few large centres with many smaller satellite settlements. Is this the intended message of the illustration? Would this same 'impression' have been apparent if instead the same symbol with a different colour/tone had been used for the two types of settlement?

A more neutral pattern is shown in Barclay's (2003, 136) map showing the distribution of henges, hengiform enclosures, cursus monuments and recumbent stone circles in Scotland (Figure 2.3). The symbols seem to have a certain superficial link to the monuments that they are depicting (round open circles = henge, square = cursus) and have a 1:1 equivalence. The map shows regional and almost mutually exclusive distribution patterns of certain monument types, although as with Ashmore's plan (Figure 2.1), these sites are by no means all contemporary. In this case, it was only the creation of the map that actually led Barclay to recognise regional patterns rather than the map depicting an already assumed pattern (pers. comm.), reinforcing the idea that maps are not necessarily designed to tell a particular story, but that patterns can be read from them that allow new or different interpretations of the past.

These three distribution maps – all focused on Scotland – employ a range of symbology strategies, ranging from the abstract to the naturalistic; and from the generalised to the specific. All depict selective forms of data – monuments – and patterns can be read into the way that the data has been depicted. This is not necessarily the aim of the mapmaker, but the power of maps and our ability to read them means than certain concepts (core / periphery; regionality) seem implicit in their design. These patterns are reinforced by the data that are excluded from the maps, but also their temporal ambiguity. It is also fair to mention that all three of these maps were produced for popular publications with the agenda to get over fairly simple distribution information to the general reader. Clearly maps can be subverted and interpreted by different kinds of readers; this may make the map more, or less, useful that intended.

BOUNDARIES

The spatial arrangements of point value symbols visually exploit another implicit understanding we have of maps. Clusters of symbols draw our eyes and we understand this as some kind of significant grouping. Partly at least this is due to the statistical limitations of distribution maps – they depict relationships so complicated that we can do nothing but simplify them. With this simplification comes the temptation to draw formally boundaries implicit in any apparently cluster. Darvill's (1987, 104) distribution map (Figure 2.4) bears comparison with Barclay's (Figure 2.3) in that they both depict the same types of sites albeit over a different geographical extents. Unlike Barclay however, Darvill has formally delimited one particular distribution. Recumbent stone circles are shown by a shaded area, establishing a fixed boundary that is only suggested in Barclay's map. This process is knows as aggregation or area conversion (Monmonier 1996, 28) and partly reflects the scale of the map and amount of data that needs to be depicted.

Boundaries are rarely depicted on archaeological distribution maps. Boundary drawing is left to the reader, based on the information presented to them. The inclusion of boundaries in archaeological maps is problematic because they are arbitrary and inflexible, and no more solid or fixed than the boundary in time between the Mesolithic and Neolithic. Boundaries represent nothing other than a known extent of a certain dataset, and did not exist in the past in the sense that we can choose to depict them. Yet attempts have been made to depict boundaries and thus zones or regions, sometimes influenced by trends in mapping and modelling in geography (Tilley 1994, 10).

Various techniques have been used, from shaded areas of different density; through to isochromatic contour lines (Childe 1957); to solid line boundaries (Burl 1969, 2); and

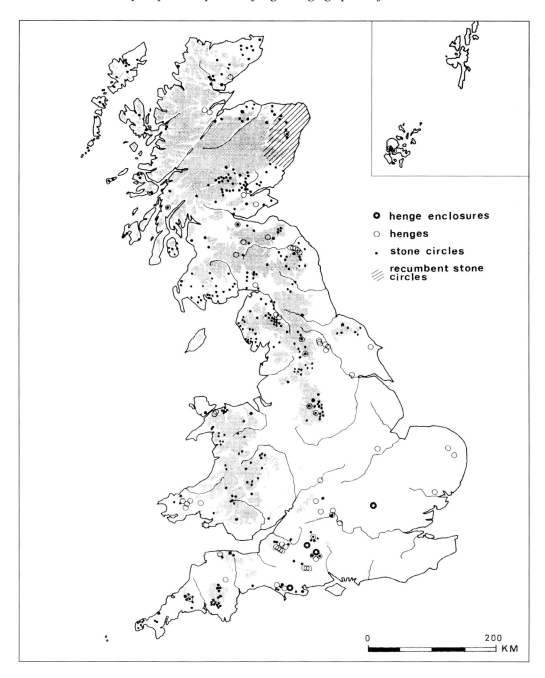

Figure 2.4 The use of shading: distribution of major henge monuments and stone circles in Britain (from Darvill 1987, 104, fig 58).

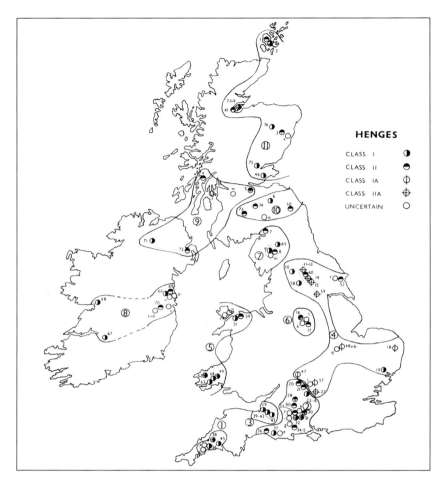

Figure 2.5 The use of fixed boundaries: henges: distribution and regional groups (from Burl 1969, 2, fig 1).

even imposed polygons or grids on top of the archaeological and topographic data (*e.g.* Renfrew 1976; Barker and Webley 1977). These conventions deny flexibility and appear to the reader to be firm and non-negotiable – a fact. Yet they no more depict social reality than an isobar on a television weather chart depicts meteorological reality. They are approximations and estimates, suggesting a particular gradiation on a sliding scale only. This plan-free information (that is, the boundaries cannot actually have a grid reference) often encourages the reader to think various things, even if the boundaries are contorted and squeezed into improbable shapes to include anomalous sites or relationships.

Burl (1969) for instance attempted to place fixed boundaries on regional traditions of henge monuments in the British Isles (Figure 2.5). Strange wobbly lines enclose land, sea

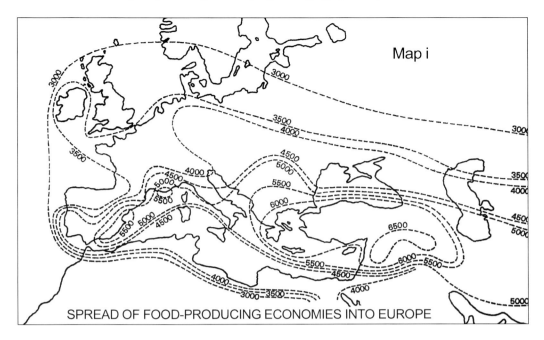

Figure 2.6 The use of notional boundaries: isochronic map showing the spread of food-producing economies into Europe (from Childe 1957, 29, map i).

and groups of supposedly superficially similar henges (based on boundary form and internal features). These boundaries are depicted as solid lines, and any outliers can be regarded as anomalous in terms of the date they were built or our archaeological interpretation. A bizarre series of symbols based on a circle renders the map, to my eye, meaningless, as there appears to be no logic in the way that regional groupings seem to transcend class.

Childe's (1957, 29) map, depicting the 'spread of food-producing economies into Europe' (Figure 2.6), was one of a number of isochronic (or isopleth) maps he deployed to describe and chart the sweep of various large-scale processes in prehistoric Europe and the Near East. In some of these, the location of the origins of agriculture are placed centrally within the box enclosing the map, reinforcing the idea of core and periphery that was explicit in the invasion models of the day. Often, Britain is located so peripherally that it is rendered distorted, seemingly sliding off the corner of the globe. The use of dotted or solid isochrons (equivalent familiar versions of this are contours on OS maps and isobars on weather charts) further creates the illusion of civilisation oozing to the north and west. This was very much central to mainstream archaeological thinking at the time, a metaphor for people and civilisation creeping in those directions (*e.g.* Childe 1935, 1940, 1946; Piggott 1954). The map in Figure 2.6 could even be read metaphorically as a contour map, with Western Europe at the bottom of the slope.

Boundaries are also important in terms of where they are actually depicted – many

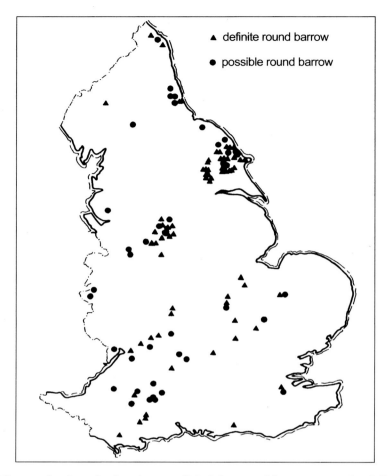

Figure 2.7 The use of scale 1: the distribution of Neolithic round barrows in England (from Harding 1997, 284, fig 3).

distribution maps amputate parts of the British Isles, and this is usually in part at least due to the perception that there is no meaningful data in the missing part(s). This may well in turn strengthen the distribution being depicted, much in the same way as a graph can be manipulated simply by not starting the x-axis at zero. Shetland is commonly lopped off (partly because it rarely fits onto the page), as is the Isle of Man. However there are other instances of losing places such as Cornwall (Figure 2.7, Harding 1987, 284), or even all of northern Britain and Ireland (Figure 2.8). Mercer's (Figure 2.8a) distribution map of known causewayed enclosures reinforces the notion that these are a southern English phenomenon (now dispelled *cf.* Darvill and Thomas 2001; Oswald *et al.* 2001; Brophy 2004). Donegore, in Northern Ireland, is depicted simply by an arrow pointing off somewhere into the Irish Sea, off the map.

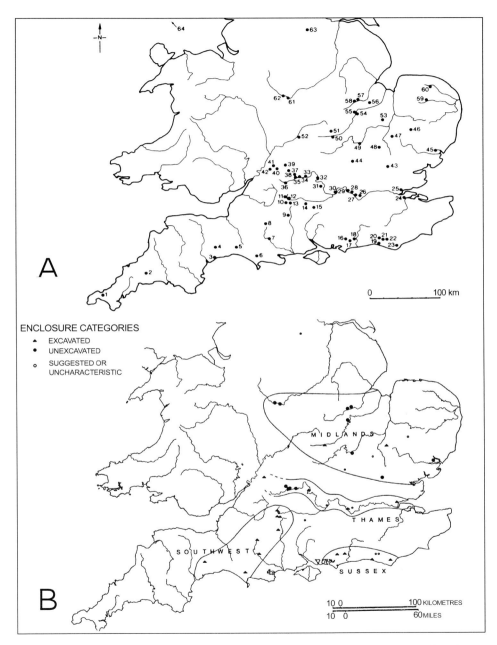

Figure 2.8 The use of scale and data: maps showing the distribution of causewayed enclosures (a) where Donegore in number 64 (from Mercer 1990, illus 1); (b) (from Palmer 1976, 172, fig 9).

DATA

If boundaries are used to frame the data and even group the data, what of the data themselves? Clearly the choice of data to be depicted is important, both in helping construct relationships and create patterns. Each distribution map is a collection of layers of data, including topographical, locational and archaeological. Some of these layers are left unacknowledged, and yet implicitly suggest a relationship with an archaeologically-derived distribution. Palmer's (1976, 172) distribution map of causewayed enclosures in southern England (Figure 2.8b) depicts different data from Mercer's map (Figure 2.8b). Palmer's map includes the coastline; modern county names; causewayed enclosure 'groupings' marked by solid boundaries; symbology relating to the survival of causewayed enclosures (cropmark / earthwork); and major rivers. The link between the causewayed enclosures and rivers is clearly made on the map, yet no other topographical features have been selected for depiction (apart from the coastline). Whether deliberate suggestion or not, the reader will assume this is a meaningful relationship.

Relationships between layers of data are often used to justify or explain distributions, like the map of flint mines across the British Isles shown in Figure 2.9 (from Barber *et al.* 1999, 2). One layer of information is chalk, another is land over 200m. The point data recorded on the map are such that one dot = one flint mine complex, and all of these are comfortably situated within the highlighted geological band. This map, from *The Neolithic Flint mines of England* (*ibid.*), depicts flint mines from across the British Isles. However, no geological information is depicted for the non-English mines (Ballygalley Hill, Den of Boddam and Skelmuir Hill), making them appear to the reader as peripheral and decontextualised. They appear to be mining nothing at all, or some generic geological background. Could not the boundaries of the flint-bearing Buchan Gravels have been included (Saville 1993)? The data selected for depiction in this particular map give the presumably unintentional impression of a core and periphery, reinforced by three 'provinces' indicated by dotted straight lines. It should be remembered that the data left out of a map can alter the meaning just as much as the data that are left in.

Data are clearly problematic when dealt with uncritically, especially when they are used to an end such as confirming, illustrating, or even making, a theory. Richards makes this point when considering Childe's approach to Skara Brae (Richards 1995, 121–122; Childe 1931). Childe's initial dating of Skara Brae as Pictish was based partly on the overlapping distribitional patterns of carved stone balls (found at Skara Brae) and Pictish symbol stones (Figure 2.10). This conclusion was the results of 'Childe's contemporary and archaeological experiences of a highly parochial Scotland' (Richards 1995, 122), where it was possible for Childe to regard this overlapping distributional patterns as proof of his relatively low opinion of northern Scottish prehistoric architecture, from Skara Brae to the brochs.

The data depicted and left off maps, then, must always be an issue for the mapmaker. Choices made at the very point of construction of the map have implications for how the map will be interpreted, and care must be exercised as the reader can only work with the selective data put before them. This is increasingly an issue with the usage and construction of GIS maps and working with data in GIS models. This has the added flexibility that layers can be turned on and turned off, so created maps may still have restrictions for the reader, but interactive maps mean that increasingly the map user can be empowered (say, through internet GIS applications) to choose for themselves what data construct the map.

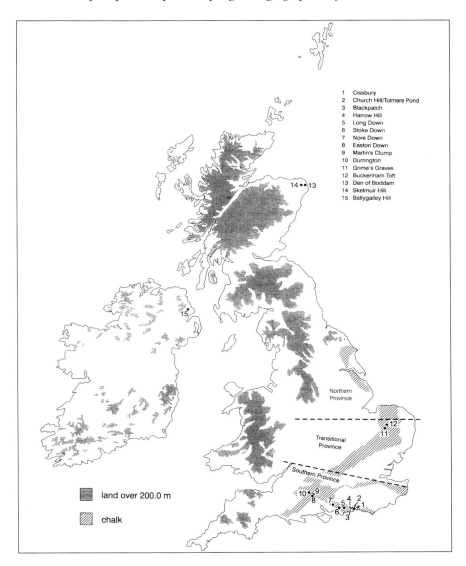

1 Cissbury
2 Church Hill/Tolmere Pond
3 Blackpatch
4 Harrow Hill
5 Long Down
6 Stoke Down
7 Nore Down
8 Easton Down
9 Martin's Clump
10 Durrington
11 Grime's Graves
12 Buckenham Toft
13 Den of Boddam
14 Skelmuir Hill
15 Ballygalley Hill

Northern Province

Transitional Province

Southern Province

land over 200.0 m

chalk

Figure 2.9 Distribution map of Neolithic flint mines of Britain and Ireland (from Barber et al. *1999, illus. 1).*

SCALES

'One of the main uses of all sorts of maps is to work out the distances between places. We can do this accurately as maps have been carefully drawn to scale'

(Kemp 1989, 10)

All maps have scales – both spatial and temporal. The conventions of scales are understood, whether appearing as a bar with shaded black and white sections, as a line, or as a written phrase (one inch to the mile, 1:10000 and so on). We expect to see scales on maps, although they are not always deemed necessary – for instance many of the figures reproduced with this paper have no scale, partly because they are not maps for measuring from, but also because it is understood that we know how big Britain, England and Scotland and so on are. This unspoken convention is rather like the understanding we have that unless told otherwise north is to the top of the page / map, and that N = north. (Both the N arrow and scale have become minimalist or even non-existent in our contemporary archaeological maps, unlike the elaborate calligraphy of earlier times (*cf.* Sumner 1988).) The spatial scale of the map has some impact on the data presented, implicitly suggesting dense or scattered distributions; and it controls the level of detail allowed (compare recumbent stone circle symbology in Figures 2.3 and 2.4).

What of the other dimension of scale that is less explicit: time? Maps have a temporal dimension, as I have hinted at with the condensed distribution data in Figures 2.1–2.4 as well as several others. Also, maps are always going out of date (Wood 1993); this is especially true of archaeological distribution maps. But there is still another temporal aspect – the points that we depict on maps have no temporal depth. They are situated in map space. Map space is both timeless and infinite. The distribution map floats uneasily in a vacuum, and we are never entirely sure whether it depicts the past, or only describes a state of knowledge at a particular point in the present, what Wood (*ibid.* 126) calls 'a perpetual, virtual past'. Distribution maps are condensed maps, 'time collapsed into space' (*ibid.* 127), rather like excavation plans and cropmark transcriptions. It is only our restricted forms of visualisation that makes these monuments, objects or places seem contemporary and unchanging.

TOWARDS ALTERNATIVE MAPPING STRATEGIES

'Studies in the Neolithic of Britain run the risk of observing a picture dominated by its frame'

(Bradley 1984, 5).

Distribution maps then are open to negotiation and exploitation. They depict local, regional, national patterns through a series of signs and conventions that we understand and interpret. Meaning is not inherent in the map, but the reader is guided visually through metaphors and signifiers, and 'reads' within the context of archaeological discourse and our socialized knowledge of maps. This is not a devious process; after all, maps are a very useful device for getting across locational information, showing changes in extents of knowledge, and can act as shorthand for complex ideas. However we should be clear that distribution maps are an uneasy marriage of non-reflective choices at the stage of designing the map, and readers who are extremely sophisticated at reading maps. The uncritical use of distribution maps leaves open the possibility for mapmakers to believe that they are neutrally depicting the archaeological record whilst map readers believe that what they are looking at is an objective document depicting some reality in the past.

Distribution maps serve a number of functions, and one of them is to show meaningful patterns in archaeological data. However, it is difficult to accept that we can 'map' complex human and social relationships with this coarse tool. Nevertheless, maps and plans are necessary parts of archaeological discourse, and the adoption of more transparent and reflective practice in the production of distribution maps is more desirable than abandoning maps altogether. More guarded use of symbols, scales and boundaries would be useful, and more interactive ways of the reader manipulating the data would be welcome, as well as the production, where possible, of alternative combinations of data. There may even be a place for different kinds of maps, breaking out of the rigid conventions discussed above.

This is certainly possible. Maps need not have any empirical or locational specificity – data can be depicted in a variety of mapping strategies, through the use of topological mapping, surrealist mappings or abstractions with no implied scale (see examples in Figures 2.11–2.12). Such maps consist of

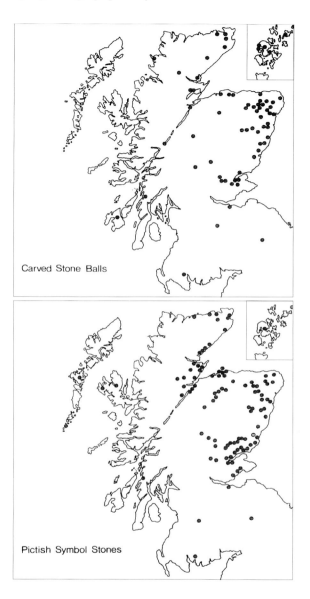

Figure 2.10 Childe's distribution 'illusion' (from Richards 1995, 119, fig 5).

transparently subjective as well as archaeological data, showing perceived patterns (not inherent in the data) or giving primacy to relationships other than spatial. Topological maps (the most familiar example being the London Underground map) are particularly useful, although untested in archaeology. 'Topology is a branch of geometric mathematics

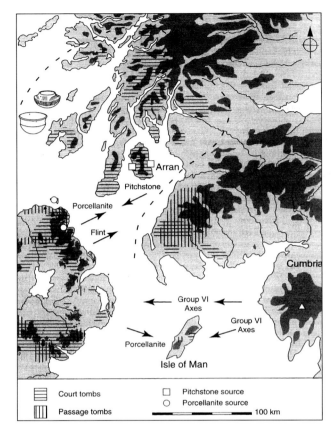

Figure 2.11 An ambiguous distribution map, depicting relationships and overlapping distributions (from Cooney 2000, 55, fig 2).

which is concerned with order, contiguity and relative position, rather than with actual linear dimensions' (Monkhouse and Wilkinson 1978, 85; my emphasis); and maps that give primacy to relationships over spatial data may offer a more realistic depiction of people's engagements with the world and ours with the data (Brophy in prep.). There are plenty of examples within ethnographic literature to suggest that our modern Western concept of mapping is not the only way to depict the world (*e.g.* Chatwin 1987; Kuchler 1993; Tilley 1994, chapter 2; Strang 1997; Ingold 2000). The inclusion of the distribution of 'natural features' on archaeological maps, for instance, may be an idea worth developing (see for instance Tilley's (1994) maps recording his phenomenological experiences (Figure 2.12), and Shanks 1992, 87).

Essentially, it seems to me that it would be useful for archaeologists to think more reflectively about the use of mapping and distribution maps in particular. Strategies that can deal with ambiguous subjective material records (Ashmore and Knapp 1999, 2) and

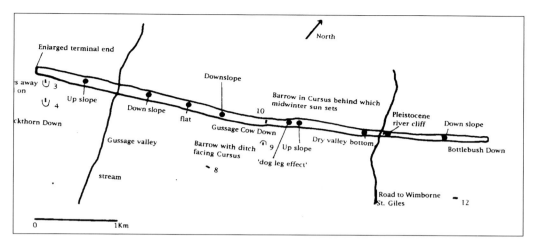

Figure 2.12 A phenomenological map including 'natural features', archaeological data and subjective observations (from Tilley 1994, 174, fig 5.15).

multiple interpretations would be a good start. Maps should be dialogues (Shanks 1992) between mapmaker and reader; but also between data and mapmaker. This is something that GIS could be very good at, but has only recently been used in this way (*e.g.* Llobera 1996; Gillings *et al.* 1999; Chapman 2003). There have been notable attempts at depicting complex inter-cutting regional traditions with traditional maps, for instance for Ireland's monument traditions (Cooney 2000, 55, and see fig. 2.11), but all too often, recent publications simply repeat, and retreat to, the maps of the past (notably Malone 2001).

In the end, archaeologists will always need to depict our ideas in some way. Diagrams and maps are vital, but should be subject to the same level of critical analysis that are now applied to other standard areas of archaeological discourse such as text (Shanks and Tilley 1987), excavation reports (Tilley 1989), the Harris matrix (Lucas 2001) and excavation (Hodder 1997). Such a critique allows us to think challenging thoughts about how we can bridge the gap between visual representation and the past. Barrett (1999) has argued that our distribution maps are meaningless because they fail to capture the temporality of our existence – they fail to depict how the past was drawn into present discourse even in prehistory, fail to show how monuments still impacted on the landscape millennia after their construction. To depict time depth and relationships as well as spatial data based on our typologies is surely the challenge.

ACKNOWLEDGEMENTS

I would like to thank Jan – a real geographer – for advice in the preparation of this paper. Thanks also to Gordon Barclay for his insightful comments and helping me to change the focus of the paper; the final version however is all down to me.

Bibliography

Anderson, J., 1886, *Scotland in pagan times: the Bronze and the Stone Ages*. Edinburgh. David Douglas.

Ashmore, W. and Knapp, A. B., 1999, *Archaeological landscapes: constructed, conceptualised and ideational*. In W. Ashmore and A. B. Knapp, 1998, 1–30.

Ashmore, W. and Knapp, A. B. (eds), 1999, *Archaeologies of landscape*. Oxford. Blackwell.

Armit, I. and Ralston, I. B. M., 2003, *The Iron Age*. In K. J. Edwards and I. B. M. Ralston, 2003, 169–194.

Ashmore, P., 1996, *Neolithic and Bronze Age Scotland*. London. Historic Scotland / Batsford.

Barber, M., Field, D. and Topping, P., 1999, *The Neolithic flint mines of England*. Swindon. English Heritage.

Barclay, G. J., 2001, 'Metropolitan' and 'Parochial'/'Core' and 'Periphery': a historiography of the Neolithic of Scotland. *Proceedings of the Prehistoric Society*, 67, 1–16.

Barclay, G. J., 2003, *The Neolithic*. In K. J. Edwards and I. B. M. Ralston, 2003, 127–150.

Barker, G. and Webley, D., 1978, Causewayed camps and earlier Neolithic economies in central southern England. *Proceedings of the Prehistoric Society*, 44, 161–185.

Bender, B., 1998, *Stonehenge: making space*, Oxford. Berg.

Barrett, J. C., 1999, *The mythical landscapes of the British Iron Age*, in W. Ashmore and A. B Knapp, 1999, 253–265.

Bradley, R., 1984, Regional systems in Neolithic Britain. In R. Bradley and J. Gardiner (eds), *Neolithic Studies: a review of some current research* (BAR British Series 133). Oxford. British Archaeological Reports. 5–14.

Brophy, K., 2004, The Searchers: the quest for causewayed enclosures in the Irish Sea area, in V Cummings and C. Fowler (eds), *The Neolithic of the Irish Sea: materiality and traditions of practice*. Oxford. Oxbow. 37–45.

Brophy, K., 2005, Not my type. Discourses in monumentality. In V. Cummings and A. Pannett (eds), *Set in stone: new approaches to Neolithic monuments in Scotland*. Oxford. Oxbow, 1–13.

Brophy, K., in prep., *Modern monuments*.

Burl, A., 1969, Henges: internal features and regional groups. *Archaeological Journal*, 126, 1–28.

Chapman, H. P., 2003, Rudston cursus 'A' – engaging with a Neolithic monument in its landscape setting using GIS. *Oxford Journal of Archaeology*, 22.4, 345–356.

Chatwin, B., 1987, *The songlines*. London. Cape.

Childe, V. G., 1931, *Skara Brae: a Pictish village in Orkney*. London. Kegan Paul, Trench and Trubner.

Childe, V. G., 1935, *The prehistory of Scotland*. London. Kegan Paul, Trench and Trubner.

Childe, V. G., 1940, *Prehistoric Scotland*. London. Historical Association.

Childe, V. G., 1946, *Scotland before the Scots*. London. Methuen.

Childe, V. G., 1947, *Prehistoric communities of the British Isles*. London. W and R Chambers.

Childe, V. G., 1957, *The dawn of European civilisation* [5th edition]. London. Paladin.

Cooney, G., 2000, Recognising regionality in the Irish Neolithic. In A. Desmond, G. Johnson, M. McCarthy, J. Sheehan and E. Shee Twohig (eds), *New agendas in Irish Prehistory*. Bray. Wordwell. 49–66.

Curwen, C., 1930, Neolithic camps. *Antiquity*, 4, 22–54.

Darvill, T., 1987, *Prehistoric Britain*. London: Batsford.

Darvill, T. and Thomas, J., 2001, *Neolithic enclosures in Atlantic Northwest Europe*. Oxford. Oxbow.

Edwards, K. J. and Ralston, I. B. M., (eds), 2003, *Scotland after the Ice Age*. Edinburgh. Edinburgh University Press.

Gillings, M., Mattingly, D. and van Dalen, J., (eds), *Geographical information systems and landscape archaeology*. Oxford. Oxbow.

Harding, J., 1997, Interpreting the Neolithic: the monuments of North Yorkshire. *Oxford Journal of Archaeology*, 16, 279–295.

Harrison, P. and Harrison, S., 1988, *Master maps with Ordnance Survey*. Southampton /Edinburgh. Ordnance Survey / Holmes McDougall.

Hodder, I., 1997, 'Always momentary, fluid and flexible': towards a reflexive excavation methodology. *Antiquity*, 71, 691–700.

Hodder, I., 1999, *The archaeological process*. Oxford. Blackwell.

Ingold, T., 2000, To journey along the way of life: maps, wayfinding and navigation. In Ingold, T., *The perception of the environment: essays on livelihood, dwelling and skill*. London. Routledge.

Kemp, R., 1989, *Investigating mapwork*. Oxford. Oxford University Press.

Kuchler, S., 1993, Landscape as memory: the mapping of process and its representation in a Melanesian society. In B. Bender (ed.), *Landscape: politics and perspectives*. Oxford. Berg. 85–106.

Llobera, M., 1996, Exploring the topography of the mind: GIS, social space and archaeology, *Antiquity*, 70, 612–622.

Lucas, G., 2001, *Critical approaches to fieldwork: contemporary and historical archaeological practice*. London. Routledge.

Malone, C., 2001, *Neolithic Britain and Ireland*. Stroud. Tempus.

Mercer, R. J. C., 1990, *Causewayed enclosures*. Princes Risborough. Shire.

Monkhouse, F. J. and Wilkinson, H. R., 1978, *Maps and diagrams: their compilation and construction*. London. Methuen and Co. Ltd.

Monmonier, M., 1996, *How to lie with maps* [2nd edition]. London. University of Chicago Press.

Oswald, A., Dyer, C. and Barber, M., 2001, *The creation of monuments: Neolithic causewayed enclosures in the British Isles*. Swindon. English Heritage.

Palmer, R., 1976, Interrupted ditch enclosures in Britain. *Proceedings of the Prehistoric Society*, 42, 161–186.

Perec, G., 1997, *Species of places and other pieces*. Harmondsworth. Penguin.

Piggott, S., 1939, Timber circles: a re-examination. *The Archaeological Journal*, 96, 193–222.

Piggott, S., 1954, *The Neolithic cultures of the British Isles*. Cambridge. Cambridge University Press.

Renfrew, C., 1976, *Before civilisation: the radiocarbon revolution and prehistoric Europe*. Harmondsworth: Penguin.

Richards, C., 1995, Vere Gordon Childe at Skara Brae and Rinyo: research and redemption. In P. Gathercote, T. H. Irving and G. Mellenish (eds), *Childe and Australia: archaeology, politics and ideas*. Queensland. University of Queensland Press. 118–127.

Saville, A., 1993, Digging for flint in prehistoric Scotland. *Glasgow Archaeological Society Bulletin*, 30, 5–7.

Shanks, M., 1992, *Experiencing the past*. London. Routledge.

Shanks, M. and Tilley, C., 1987, *Re-constructing archaeology*. Cambridge. Cambridge University Press.

Sharples, N., 1992, Aspects of regionalisation in the Scottish Neolithic. In N. Sharples and A. Sheridan (eds), *Vessels for the ancestors*. Edinburgh: Edinburgh University Press. 322–331.

Southern, T., 1997, *Dr Strangelove*. London. Bloomsbury.

Strang, V., 1997, *Uncommon ground. Cultural landscapes and environmental values*. Oxford. Berg.

Sumner, H., 1988, *The ancient earthworks of Cranborne Chase*. Gloucester. Sutton.

Tilley, C., 1989, Archaeology as theatre. *Antiquity*, 63, 275–280.

Tilley, C., 1994, *A phenomenology of landscape*. Oxford. Berg.

Thomas, J., 1998, Towards a regional Geography of the Neolithic. In M. Edwards and C. Richards (eds), *Understanding the Neolithic of north-western Europe*. Glasgow. Cruithne Press. 37–59.

Thomas, J., 1999, *Understanding the Neolithic*. London. Routledge.

Wood, D., 1993, *The power of maps*. London. Routledge.

Chapter 3

Corn grinding in southern England: what can the querns tell us?

Fiona Roe

INTRODUCTION

Neolithic studies are not usually approached from the viewpoint of querns and the materials used to make them. However, stone is on the whole a good survivor, and can in addition often be traced to a source, so that it has potential for revealing some of the secrets of the prehistoric past. This paper attempts a study of four areas, to see what may be learnt from this different viewpoint. As more querns become available for examination, they may be able to tell us something about the Neolithic way of life, depending on the varieties of quernstone that were available in different areas. There were four main ways in which lithic materials were used during the Neolithic period: for flaked artefacts, for axes, for other implements including querns, and as a construction medium. This study concentrates on types of stone that were suitable for grinding foodstuffs, especially cereals, though other possibilities need not be discounted.

Earlier publications have tended to suggest that, typically, local stone was used for saddle querns. This is certainly true of Windmill Hill, where abundant sarsen was available near to the site. There was no need to transport it more than a mile or so, resulting in some particularly thick 'saucer' querns of robust appearance (Smith 1965, 120 and fig. 42). Sarsen is a good grinding material, and its use for saddle querns must have been general practice in Neolithic Wiltshire. In Cornwall too local quernstone was available, exemplified by finds from Carn Brea. Here saddle querns and rubbers were not numerous, but were made from Cornish granite, elvan and tuff (Smith 1981). The finds from these two sites could have given the impression that there was not much more to be said on the subject, but recent studies have begun to widen the picture. By chance rather than design, all four examples described here come from southern England. This does at least have the advantage of clarity, since there are fewer Pleistocene deposits in the region to confuse the issue of whether stone was transported by ice or by human agency.

DISCUSSION OF QUERNS FOUND IN FOUR DIFFERENT AREAS

In the Cotswolds, the first area to be considered, the underlying rock is predominantly Jurassic limestone. This would not have been an ideal grinding material, and any querns made from it would probably have worn down too quickly. There is only limited evidence from Iron Age sites that limestone was sometimes used for querns (Roe, in prep. a). Any fragments of Neolithic limestone querns could well have evaded recognition, and no examples are currently known.[1] Pieces of imported quernstone, however, stand out well. These are now known from three Neolithic sites around Cirencester, and are all made from the same stone, a Silurian gritstone from May Hill in the north-west of Gloucestershire (Lawson 1955).

The finds come from an area in which funerary monuments could be built out of the local limestone, and part of a well-worn saddle quern was built into the cairn at the Burn Ground, a Cotswold-Severn long barrow near Northleach, Gloucestershire (Grimes 1960, 75). This site is some 40 km from May Hill. The second find is from Duntisbourne Grove, near Cirencester, Gloucestershire, and came from one of a group of Neolithic pits, which contained worked flints and fragments of two rubbers of May Hill sandstone (Mudd *et al.* 1999, 20). Another pit in the same group yielded an unworked flake of Upper Old Red Sandstone, and this has a source in the Forest of Dean (Roe 1999a, 419). Cereals were also recorded (op cit., 22). The flint must have been imported as well as the quernstone, and probably came from the chalk downs to the south-east (Saville 1982).

Only 3.6 km from the Burn Ground, the chambered tomb at Hazleton covered the remains of a midden (Saville 1990), and this produced fragments of May Hill sandstone. The specialist reports in this excavation report have presented a broader picture than is often possible for this period. Cereals were grown here (Straker 1990, 215), and there are further imported materials. It is suggested that some of the clay used for potting came from the Lias (Smith and Darvill 1990, 141), and the Liassic outcrop would have had to be crossed on a north-west route going towards May Hill. At least some of the flint, and some sarsen, came from the chalk downs in the opposite direction (Saville 1990, 154 and 176), while the polished flint axes may have had a separate, more distant, source or sources (op. cit., 165).

These few sites are not sufficient to claim a regional group. However some further clues are provided by distribution maps of sites and finds of axes in the area, since these appear to cluster on the well drained soils of the Cotswolds, including the area that the querns come from (Darvill 1987, 35, 41 and 47). What happened next is also a point of interest, since the use of May Hill sandstone did not die out, and by the middle Iron Age it was being used for saddle querns all over the Cotswolds (Roe 1999b). The Neolithic here appears to have seen the start of a very conservative tradition of quernstone use, and this is a pattern that is repeated elsewhere.

The two causewayed camps on Hambledon Hill in Dorset, the main causewayed enclosure and the Stepleton enclosure, represent a somewhat different set of circumstances from those discussed above, but quern fragments were found here too, and in considerable numbers. These came from both pits and ditches, and were also found in the ditches of one of the long barrows. The sites are on chalk, where again imported stone is readily identified, and no fewer than 77 worked fragments were retrieved, with numerous unworked pieces of quern material (Roe, in prep. b). The use of sarsen could have been predicted here (Bowen and Smith 1977, 188 and fig. 1), and indeed did occur, but only accounted for around 11% of the quern materials, a smaller proportion than might have been expected (Roe, in prep. b). About one third of the querns were made from the local Upper Greensand, which came from up to 13 km away (Bristow *et al.* 1995). Another 24% of the quern materials were purple Tertiary sandstone, from the heathlands of south Dorset (Arkell 1947), and this heathstone occurred particularly in the Stepleton enclosure. In the main causewayed enclosure, however, Old Red Sandstone was preferred, even though the source on the Mendips was some 40 km away to the north (Green and Welch 1965).

Other contributions to the main Hambledon Hill report help to fill out the picture. Cereals, mainly emmer and barley, were present (Jones and Legge, in prep.). Some potting materials came from areas that could have been visited while en route to and from sources of quernstone. The Jurassic limestone that was used for some temper (Darvill, in prep.) could have been collected on the way to the Mendips, while clay with iron rich pellets (op. cit.) probably came from the same area as the heathstone. The gabbroic tempered wares came from a more distant Cornish source (op. cit.), as did most of the stone axes (Smith, in prep.). The flintwork, however, appears to be mainly of local origin, supplemented by some Portland chert, while Chesil Beach, not far from Portland, could have been the source of at least some of the flint pebbles used as hammerstones (Saville, in prep.).

What all this may mean will no doubt continue to be debated in years to come. One interpretation could be that we are beginning to see two, or maybe even three groups from different areas coming together on Hambledon Hill, but using two separate causewayed enclosures. Each of these collections of people seems to have had their preferred materials, both for querns and for other artefacts. These goods must on occasion have been exchanged, so that in archaeological terms the picture is now somewhat blurred, although the general pattern is still preserved.

The territory, if such it can be called, of those preferring Old Red Sandstone as a quern material, may have extended, very approximately, between Hambledon Hill and the Mendips. This would encompass finds of a complete Old Red Sandstone quern and some fragments from early Neolithic pits that are part of the South Cadbury environs project (Tabor 2004; Peter Leach pers. comm.). Another Old Red Sandstone quern came from a pit with earlier Neolithic pottery at Camerton (Wedlake 1958, 19; Shaffrey 2006). Those favouring heathstone as a quern material may have been operating mainly to the south of Hambledon Hill. Two querns made from this coarse sandstone came from earlier Neolithic pits at Pamphill, Dorset (Addison 1989, 27). The area covered by Cranborne Chase could possibly represent further people who used Hambledon Hill as a meeting place, bringing with them the ubiquitous sarsen querns, which were also recorded at the Whitesheet causewayed enclosure (Healy 2004). They probably also used querns made from Upper Greensand, which, apart from the Hambledon finds, are at present mainly known from Bronze Age sites in the area. Further sarsen querns from early Neolithic contexts are also known from south of Hambledon Hill, at Maiden Castle (Patchett 1943, 322; Laws 1991, 230). As was found in the Cotswolds, the Neolithic use of quern materials in Dorset and Somerset was the beginning of long traditions. Recent work on the South Cadbury Environs project has demonstrated the use of both Upper Greensand and Mendip Old Red Sandstone during the Bronze Age (Tabor 2004), while many of the Iron Age querns from Cadbury Castle were again made from similar Mendip Old Red Sandstone (Roe 2000, 263). Heathstone also had a long life as a quern material, and was found, for example, at Hengistbury Head (Laws 1987).

Neolithic occupation at the Eton Rowing Lake near Dorney in Buckinghamshire was situated upon gravels of the middle Thames valley (Dewey and Bromehead 1915, 69), and here a midden has produced quern fragments along with numerous other finds (Roe, forthcoming). The querns are all very fragmentary, as was the case in the Hazleton midden (Saville 1990). Sarsen appears to have been the main quern material, but has not always survived very well, particularly as any broken quern fragments tend to have been subsequently burnt. Pecked surfaces provide clues as to use, and these are very similar to surfaces prepared for grinding at Windmill Hill (Smith 1965, 123). The sarsen at Eton probably came from Chobham Common, 12 km south of the site (Dewey and Bromehead 1915, 58). This was supplemented by some of the larger quartzite and quartzitic sandstone cobbles from the local Thames gravels, which were utilised among other things for grain rubbers, while a little Tertiary sandstone was also put to use.

A fuller picture of the use of resources around Eton is becoming available as post-excavation work proceeds. Cereals, in the form of emmer and barley, were being grown (Robinson, forthcoming). Flint came mostly from the local Thames gravels, although the flint axes may well have come from further away (Lamdin-Whymark, forthcoming and pers. comm.). Stone axes were few in number, but these and a shafthole implement came from north Wales and northern England (Roe, forthcoming).

The finds at Eton are paralleled by ones from the nearby causewayed enclosure at Staines, where sarsen was also extensively used (Robertson-Mackay 1987, 118 and fiche). Worked sarsen is also known from a Neolithic context at Runnymede Bridge (Higbee 1996, 165). At Staines there is a suggestion that some non-local quern materials were also being utilised, and these were obtained from the greensand around 32 km to the south (op. cit.). At Eton, greensand was only recorded in the form of a hammerstone made from a cherty variety (Lamdin-Whymark, forthcoming), while none of the fragments found here of carstone from the Lower Greensand Folkestone Beds retained working traces.

These three sites comprise barely more than the beginnings of a regional group, but further potential exists in the Neolithic stone awaiting examination from Runnymede Bridge (Needham 1985 and pers. comm.). In this area it appears that greensands were first systematically imported during the Bronze Age, perhaps following on from some tentative Neolithic exploitation at Eton and Staines. Both Lodsworth and Bargate stone are known, for example, from Bronze Age contexts at Runnymede Bridge (Humphrey 1996, 168). Sarsen querns also continued to be widely used during the Bronze Age and later, and were found, for example, together with greensand querns at the late Bronze/early Iron Age site at Carshalton (Adkins and Needham 1985, 38).

The fourth area for discussion from the point of view of quern use is the upper Thames valley in Oxfordshire. The finds from Yarnton are still being studied, so any suggestions as to interpretation made here are provisional. Neolithic activity here took place on the Thames gravels and floodplain (Richardson *et al.* 1946, 113). The context types are varied and include an old ground surface with possible elements of a midden, enclosures, a rectangular structure, ditches, pit groups, post holes and burials (Hey 1997 and pers. comm.). The difference here is that comparatively few quern fragments were found (Roe, in prep. c). As at Eton, cobbles from the river gravels could be used as grain rubbers, and a fragment of one made from quartzitic sandstone came from a Grooved Ware pit. Local quernstone was available in the form of Lower Calcareous Grit from the Corallian beds, and this could have been obtained a few miles from Yarnton, possibly from nearby Wytham Hill, or else from around Cumnor (Arkell 1947b, 89). This sandstone was used for a saddle quern fragment from the old ground surface, which produced finds of early to late Neolithic and early Bronze Age date. A sarsen rubber fragment came from the same deposit, while another worked fragment was found in a hearth dump that also contained Peterborough pottery. There are records of sarsen boulders occurring in Oxfordshire (Richardson *et al.*, 1946, 113; Arkell 1947b, 184), and these could account for some sarsen querns found in the area. However it seems very likely that flint was procured from the chalk downs which lie some 22.5 km to the south of Yarnton, since it was barely available from the gravels in the area. If expeditions were being made to the downs, it would have been feasible to bring back some sarsen together with the flint (Osborne White 1907, 119). Some chalk was also taken to Yarnton, where it has occurred mainly in beaker contexts, but was also used to temper a Grooved Ware pottery bowl (Barclay, in prep. and pers. comm.).

The tendency of sarsen to become friable when burnt, as demonstrated by the small worked fragment from Eton, might partly account for the few quern fragments recorded from Yarnton. However, very few charred cereals were found here, despite extensive sieving (Robinson 2000, 86), and it seems that growing and processing corn crops was not a priority on the floodplain. More probably the main activity here was seasonal grazing, mainly of cattle, on rich grass meadows (Hey 1997, 109). Most of the growing and grinding of corn must have been taking place elsewhere, wherever those not caring for the animals had their other, though possibly not permanent, living quarters. The Yarnton folk also acquired some stone axes from distant sources in Cornwall and north Wales.

Querns made from the same materials as those found at Yarnton are known from other Neolithic sites in Oxfordshire. Lower Calcareous Grit was used at the Abingdon causewayed enclosure (Avery 1982, 42), and also occurred in a Grooved Ware pit at Barrow Hills, Radley (Roe 1999c, 82). Sarsen must have been widely used, as in other areas, and was better preserved by re-use in the chambered tomb at Wayland's Smithy (Whittle 1991, 87 and fig. 11). Lower Greensand has not been recorded at Yarnton before the Bronze Age, when some quernstone from Culham was imported in addition to the materials already in use. As in the areas considered above, in Oxfordshire the use of certain quern materials in early prehistoric times was to be the start of long traditions, and in Oxfordshire these were only to change with the introduction of rotary querns to the area (Roe, in prep. d).

CONCLUSIONS

The sites and context types considered in this brief survey have been varied, and include causewayed camps, a defended hilltop, chambered tombs and an earthen long barrow, middens, ditches and pits, and even a hearth dump. In all four areas there has been evidence for the grinding of corn, provided both by finds of quern fragments, and of cereal remains. The need for good quernstone must have been universal across southern England, and good quern materials were identified early on in the Neolithic. These then continued in use for a few thousand years, sometimes with the addition of further materials in the Bronze Age. Procurement strategies may often have been linked with those for obtaining supplies of other essential goods, particularly flint, but sometimes even clay and temper for potting. Some querns were transported up to 40 km, and it must have been necessary to walk these distances, perhaps with a stone slab resting on the shoulder. Other possible methods of transporting saddle querns might have been by using sledges, or panniers on either ponies or oxen, or even with the quern resting in a sling carried by two people. We can only guess at how it was done, but whatever the answer, it cannot have been easy, and would explain the relatively small size of Neolithic querns, compared to Iron Age ones. A complete example from Wayland's Smithy is only some 330 mm in length (Whittle 1991, 87 and fig. 11, no. 10).

Stone axes were acquired in all the four areas considered above, and in all cases they had been carried distances well in excess of 40 km. Flint axes too were often brought long distances. The ways in which these axes were distributed may well have been different from the mechanisms used to acquire quernstone, since, being a good deal smaller than querns, they could be carried more easily. Maybe a dozen or so axes could have been fitted into a knapsack, and then taken to wherever they were needed. They may, too, have played a part in specialised exchange systems (Bradley and Edmonds 1993, 12), whereas querns, perhaps, had more utilitarian connotations, linked to a basic need to provide food. They were, besides, part of procurement activities in delimited territories that need not have been more than about 80 km across.

There must have been local paths or trackways leading to the key source areas for quern materials and other goods. Places that were regularly journeyed to would have formed part of the familiar territory of a community (Bradley 2000), and must have been every bit as important for establishing local identity as the fields, buildings, barrows and causewayed camps. The people inhabiting each of the four areas considered above would have developed strong links, not only with their immediate surroundings, including the soil they cultivated, but also with the local geology, particularly in places where it could supply them with lithic materials that could be utilised. In each area a certain kind of regional loyalty must have developed, a sense of place that provided no good reason to move elsewhere. This does not necessarily imply sedentism, as there would always have been the freedom to move around within a chosen area. Moving outside this area, where the usual local supply networks were not in place, could have been a stressful experience. It would, surely, have been far better to remain in much the same area, where supplies were reasonably secure, and to continue to use the established trackways. This, if the evidence from the querns is to be believed, could be more or less what happened, with a very conservative element developing, as far as stone use was concerned. Pottery styles could come and go, and flint tools eventually became redundant, but the same quern materials continued in use for a few thousand years.

Attempts have already been made to define regional Neolithic groups using causewayed camps as a starting point (Oswald *et al.* 2001). It was concluded that 'sources of more mundane resources may offer a more reasonable impression of the extent of the territories exploited by the groups who build and used causewayed enclosures' (op. cit., 199), and indeed pottery can, for example, provide useful indications of regional differences. The evidence from querns in the areas described above is limited so far. However, with ever improving methods of recording worked stone, further finds could be expected to become available and fill in more details. Querns from other areas such as Kent and Sussex also have potential for more detailed study. Little attempt has been made here to consider chronological differences in any detail, and these may not have a great deal of relevance when dealing with long and conservative traditions. The same regional divisions, according to the type of quernstone in use, can be seen to continue through to the Iron Age. By this time some tribal groups are known by name. Regional boundaries may have shifted to and fro over the centuries, but the core areas probably remained basically the same. All this began to change with the introduction of rotary querns during the later Iron Age, since in some areas, particularly Oxfordshire, different quern materials were apparently needed to accompany the new technology. The old ways of life were changed for ever with the arrival of the Romans, since entirely new ways of distributing quern and millstone materials long distance were introduced, and new roads were built to take the growing amount of traffic.

ACKNOWLEDGEMENTS

I am very grateful to Tim Allen, Alistair Barclay, Frances Healy and Gill Hey for many useful discussions and for reading through my draft manuscript. However I take all responsibility for the ideas put forward here.

Note

1. Since this was written in 2002, limestone quern fragments from the Ascott-under-Wychwood long barrow, Oxfordshire, have been published in D. Benson and A. Whittle (eds) 2007, *Building Memories: The Neolithic Cotswold Long Barrow at Ascott-under-Wychwood, Oxfordshire*, Oxford, Oxbow Books, 315 and fig. 13.1.

Bibliography

Addison, P., 1989, Excavation of Neolithic and Bronze Age pits and a Section of Roman Road on a Pipeline near Lodge Farm, Pamphill, Dorset. *Proceedings of the Dorset Natural History and Archaeological Society*, 111, 15–29.
Adkins, L. and Needham, S., 1985, *New Research on a late Bronze Age Enclosure at Queen Mary's Hospital, Carshalton*. Surrey Archaeological Collections, 76, 11–50.
Allen, T., Barclay, A., Mortimer, S. and Welsh, K., forthcoming, *The Archaeology of a Middle Thames Landscape. The Eton Rowing Lake Project and the Maidenhead, Windsor and Eton Flood Alleviation Scheme, Volume 1: The early Prehistory*. Oxford. Oxford Archaeology.
Arkell, W. J., 1947a, *The Geology of the Country around Weymouth, Swanage, Corfe and Lulworth* (Geological Survey Memoir for Sheets 327, 328, 329). London. HMSO.
Arkell, W. J., 1947b, *The Geology of Oxford*, Oxford. Clarendon Press.
Avery, M., 1982, The Neolithic Causewayed Camp, Abingdon. In H. J. Case and A. W. R. Whittle (eds), *Settlement patterns in the Oxford Region: excavations at the Abingdon causewayed enclosure and other sites* (CBA. Research Report No 44). London. CBA. 10–50.
Barclay, A., in prep., The pottery. In G. Hey *et al.* in prep.
Bowen, H. C. and Smith, I. F., 1977, Sarsen Stone in Wessex: The Society's first investigations in the evolution of the landscape project. *Antiquaries Journal*, 57, 185–196.
Bradley, R., 2000, *An archaeology of natural places*. London. Routledge.
Bradley, R. and Edmonds, M., 1993, *Interpreting the axe trade: production and exchange in Neolithic Britain*. Cambridge. Cambridge University Press.
Bristow, C. R., Barton, C. M., Freshney, E. C., Wood, C. J., Evans, D. J., Cox, D. M., Ivimey-Cook, H. C. and Taylor, R. T., 1995, *Geology of the Country around Shaftsbury* (British Geological Survey, Memoir for Sheet 313). London. HMSO.
Darvill, T. C., 1987, *Prehistoric Gloucestershire*. Gloucester. Alan Sutton and Gloucester County Library.

Darvill, T. C., in prep., A Petrological analysis of the Ceramic Fabrics represented among the Neolithic pottery. In R. Mercer and F. Healy, in prep.

Dewey, H., and Bromehead, C. E. N., 1915, *The Geology of the Country around Windsor and Chertsey* (Memoirs of the Geological Survey, England and Wales. Explanation of Sheet 269). London. HMSO.

Green, G. W. and Welch, F. B. A., 1965, *Geology of the Country around Wells and Cheddar* (Institute of Geological Sciences, Memoir for Sheet 280). London. HMSO.

Grimes, W. F., 1960, *Excavations on Defence Sites 1939–1945. I: Mainly Neolithic to Bronze Age*. London. HMSO.

Healy, F., 2004, Ground stone. In M. N. Rawlings, M. J. Allen and F. Healy, *Investigation of the Whitesheet Down environs 1989–90: Neolithic causewayed enclosure and Iron Age settlement, Wiltshire Archaeological and Natural History Magazine* (Wiltshire Studies), 97, 144–196.

Hey, G., 1997, Neolithic Settlement at Yarnton, Oxfordshire. In P. Topping (ed.), *Neolithic Landscapes* (Neolithic Studies Group Seminar Papers 2). Oxford. Oxbow. 100–111.

Hey, G., in prep., *Yarnton Volume 3: Neolithic and Bronze Age Settlement and Landscape*. Oxford. Oxford Archaeology.

Higbee, L., 1996, Imported stone: morphology and utilisation. In S. Needham and T. Spence, *Refuse and Disposal at Area 16, East Runnymede* (Runnymede Research Excavations, Volume 2). London. British Museum Press. 165–8.

Humphrey, S., 1996, Petrology of selected stone samples. In S. Needham and T. Spence, *Refuse and Disposal at Area 16, East Runnymede* (Runnymede Research Excavations, Volume 2). London. British Museum Press. 168–9.

Jones, G. and Legge, T., in prep., Evaluating the role of cereal cultivation in the Neolithic charred plant remains. In R. Mercer and F. Healy, in prep.

Lamdin-Whymark, H., forthcoming, The flint. In T. Allen *et al.*, forthcoming.

Laws, K., 1987, Quernstones, in B. Cunliffe, *Hengistbury Head, Dorset. Volume 1: The Prehistoric and Roman Settlement, 3500 BC–AD 500*. Oxford. Oxford University Committee for Archaeology. 167–71.

Laws, K., 1991, The foreign stone. In N. M. Sharples, *Maiden Castle: Excavations and field survey 1985–6* (English Heritage Archaeological Report No 19), London. English Heritage. 229–33.

Lawson, J. D., 1955, The Geology of the May Hill Inlier, *Quarterly Journal of the Geological Society*, 111, 85–116.

Mercer, R. and Healy, F., in prep., *Hambledon Hill, Dorset, England: Excavation and survey of a Neolithic monument complex and its surrounding landscape*. Swindon. English Heritage.

Mudd, A., Williams, R. J., and Lupton, A., 1999, *Excavations alongside Roman Ermin Street, Gloucestershire and Wiltshire. The archaeology of the A419/A417 Swindon to Gloucester Road Scheme*. Oxford. Oxford Archaeological Unit.

Needham, S. F., 1985, Neolithic and Bronze Age settlement on the buried flood plains of Runnymede, *Oxford Journal of Archaeology*, 4, 125–37.

Osborne White, H. J., 1907, *The Geology of the Country around Hungerford and Newbury* (Memoirs of the Geological Survey, England and Wales. Explanation of Sheet 267). London. HMSO.

Oswald, A., Dyer, C. and Barber, M., 2001, *The Creation of Monuments: Neolithic Causewayed Enclosures in the British Isles*, Swindon. English Heritage.

Patchett, F. M., 1943, Querns. In R. E. M. Wheeler, *Maiden Castle, Dorset* (Reports of the Research Committee of the Society of Antiquaries of London No XII). Oxford. Oxford University Press. 321–329.

Richardson, L., Arkell, W. J. and Dines, H. G., 1946, *Geology of the Country around Witney* (Memoir of the Geological Survey of Great Britain. Explanation of Sheet 236). London. HMSO.

Robertson-Mackay, R., 1987, The Neolithic causewayed enclosure at Staines, Surrey: excavations 1961–63, *Proceedings of the Prehistoric Society*, 53, 23–128.

Robinson, M. A., 2000, Further consideration of Neolithic charred cereals, fruit and nuts. In A. S. Fairbairn (ed.), *Plants in Neolithic Britain and Beyond* (Neolithic Studies Group Seminar Papers 5). Oxford. Oxbow. 85–90.

Robinson, M. A., forthcoming, Charred Plant Remains. In T. Allen *et al.*, forthcoming.

Roe, F., 1999a, The Worked Stone. In A. Mudd, R. J. Williams, and A. Lupton, 415–21.

Roe, F., 1999b, Quernstones. In C. Parry, Iron Age, Romano-British and Medieval Occupation at Bishop's Cleeve, Gloucestershire: excavations at Gilder's Paddock 1989 and 1990–1. *Transactions of the Bristol and Gloucester Archaeological Society*, 117, 109–110.

Roe, F., 1999c, Worked Stone. In A. Barclay and C. Halpin, *Excavations at Barrow Hills, Radley, Oxfordshire. Volume I: The Neolithic and Bronze Age Monument Complex* (Thames Valley Landscapes Volume 11). Oxford. Oxford Archaeological Unit. 82.

Roe, F., 2000, Worked stone. In J. C. Barrett, P. W. M. Freeman and A. Woodward, *Cadbury Castle, Somerset: The later prehistoric and early historic archaeology* (English Heritage Archaeological Report 20). Swindon. English Heritage. 262–269.

Roe, F., forthcoming, Worked stone. In T. Allen *et al.*, forthcoming.

Roe, F., in prep. a, The Worked Stone, in *Gloucestershire County Council Archaeological Service, Report on Excavations at Bourton-on-the-Water Primary School, Gloucestershire*.

Roe, F., in prep. b, Worked stone other than axes and adzes. In R. Mercer and F. Healy, in prep.

Roe, F., in prep. c, Worked stone. In G. Hey *et al.* in prep.

Roe, F., in prep. d, Worked Stone. In G. Hey *et al. Yarnton Volume 2: Iron Age and Roman Settlement and Landscape*. Oxford. Oxford Archaeology.

Saville, A., 1982, Carrying Cores to Gloucestershire: some thoughts on lithic resource exploitation, *Lithics: The Newsletter of the Lithics Study Society*, 3, 25–8.

Saville, A., 1990, *Hazleton North: The excavation of a Neolithic long cairn of the Cotswold-Severn group* (English Heritage Archaeological Report No 13). Gloucestershire. HMBC(E).

Saville, A., in prep., Report on worked flint. In R. Mercer and F. Healy, in prep.

Shaffrey, R. L., 2006, *Grinding and Milling: A study of Romano-British querns and millstones made from Old Red Sandstone*, Oxford, British Archaeological Reports 409.

Smith, I. F., 1965, *Windmill Hill and Avebury: Excavations by Alexander Keiller 1925–1939*. Oxford. Clarendon Press.

Smith, I. F., 1981, Stone Artefacts. In R. Mercer, Excavations at Carn Brea, Illogan, Cornwall – a Neolithic fortified complex of the Third Millennium. *Cornish Archaeology*, 20, 153–60.

Smith, I. F., in prep., Stone axes and adzes. In R. Mercer, and F. Healy, in prep.

Smith, I. F. and Darvill, T. C., 1990, The prehistoric pottery. In A. Saville, 141–152.

Straker, V., 1990, Carbonised plant macrofossils. In A. Saville, 215–8.

Tabor, R., (ed.), 2004, *South Cadbury Environs Project interim fieldwork report, 2002–03*, University of Bristol.

Wedlake, W. J., 1958, *Excavations at Camerton, Somerset*, Camerton Excavation Club.

Whittle, A., 1991, Wayland's Smithy, Oxfordshire: Excavations at the Neolithic Tomb in 1962–63 by R. J. C. Atkinson and S. Piggott, *Proceedings of the Prehistoric Society*, 57 part 2, 61–101.

Chapter 4

From ritual to riches – the route to individual power in later Neolithic Eastern Yorkshire?

Roy Loveday

The work of Manby (1974, 1975 and 1979), Kinnes (1979) and Pierpoint (1980) delineated a distinctive society in Later Neolithic Eastern Yorkshire characterised by the production of a range of elaborate artefacts that, in greater or lesser numbers accompanied individual interments under round barrows. Since this contrasted markedly with contemporary Wessex, Thorpe and Richards (1984) argued that divergent social strategies were evidenced: in the south an individual-subsuming ritual authority structure centred upon monuments; in Eastern Yorkshire an individual-enhancing prestige goods economy centred on the monopolisation of production and circulation of wealth items. This bimodal picture of the British Later Neolithic remains a cornerstone of explanation (*e.g.* Clarke *et al.* 1985; Bradley 1990, 68–70).

Nevertheless there are problems. Prestige goods economies are dependent upon a flow of new, exotic material, yet in Eastern Yorkshire, although 'foreign' Group VI stone axes were present in abundance, they were neither accorded high status (Manby 1979, 72) nor prized as grave goods (Kinnes 1979). Instead these were of local flint and jet. Nor can the notion of prolonged sequential introduction of new types to counter emulation by lower lineages be sustained: Pitts (1996) has questioned the integrity of the York hoard with its barbed and tanged arrowhead, and the few dates centre some 500 years in advance of the Beaker phenomenon. Equally problematic is the lack of dislocation from major ritual monuments. On the contrary, the majority of the artefacts in question are to be found within an area centred around Rudston (Pierpoint 1980) where the greatest cursus complex in northern Britain and the tallest standing stone in the country are located.

Addressing these problems Edmonds (1995, 1998) has questioned the exclusive correlation of elaborate artefacts with the concept of prestige goods, postulating instead a continuum of use in which they operated as tokens of identity and value. Valuable as this is in explaining wider patterns of elaborate artefact production, it appears too passive a mechanism to explain the transformation in Eastern Yorkshire where axes/adzes and antler maceheads achieve a greater consistency as grave accompaniments than do items of archery equipment in the Early Beaker 'package'.

Why then, and on what basis, was an individual-enhancing trajectory initiated in Eastern Yorkshire rather than in Wessex? In pursuit of an answer that accommodates non-exotic raw material, a potentially short time scale and a ritual mechanism, we need to interrogate again the primary evidence: the artefacts and the focal ritual complex.

THE ARTEFACTS

The innovations to the artefact repertoire are characterised by labour-intensive production that carried techniques of flaking and grinding well beyond functional necessity. Factors, which determined their size, form and finish, must be counted as critical therefore.

Polished rectangular knives

Despite a shared preoccupation with flatness and parallel-sided/convex ended form, these have been classified as two distinct types: type I polished flake knives and type IV discoidal knives.

Manby's type I polished flake knives (1974, 113–5) occur with burials at Duggleby Howe and Aldro C75. By virtue of the thinness of the flakes on which they have been produced they appear as extravagently broad examples of flake knives found with Later Neolithic burials at Aldro 94, Liff's Low, Radley, and Stanton Harcourt. Their extravagance is underlined by the fact that only four were recorded in Manby's total of 63 polished flake knives from Northern England.

Clark (1928) classed the larger and thicker polished rectangular knives as type IV in his discoidal series. Yet, while most discoidal knives possess a blunted base to ease grip or hafting, type IV have edges equally ground, or sharp ends but relatively blunt parallel sides. A wide parallel-sided knife would be awkward to use, one where the cutting edges lay at both ends, absurdly so. Functional development from types I–III seems improbable. Additionally type IV knives are frequently significantly thinner than the rest of the series and appear to be alone in exhibiting examples of total polishing carried to the level of removing all evidence of flake scars (Figure 4.1). Although the little dating evidence suggests a later, Grooved Ware horizon (an atypically small, irregular and partially polished specimen from Carnaby Top 12: Manby 1974, 29–30), an apparent production site nearby at North Dale (Lewis 1987; Durden 1995; Earnshaw 1995; Green pers. comm.) returned a low general incidence of oblique arrowheads (12) but a high incidence of chisel (42) and leaf forms (38 + 17 fragmentary). Additionally 10 leaf shaped arrowhead roughouts indicate production on the site. Although the material clearly represents a huge palimpsest, coincidence of distribution might suggest knife production was contemporary with earlier rather than later arrowhead types.

If identical morphological objectives (which extended well beyond the normal developmental parameters of flint technology) operated in the production of both knife types, identical stimuli might also be suggested. Extreme difficulty of production, lavish attention to polishing which accorded no technological advantage and lack of obvious hafting and display potential, argues for a compelling prototype. Wood and leather might easily be cut to a rectangular shape but neither seems likely to inspire such a level of copying, while anything else might be expected to survive in the record. Casting the net wider produces an almost exact parallel – the rectangular copper flat axe.

This type is rare in the west but widespread in central and south-eastern Europe and has been recorded as far north as Denmark (Novotná 1970; Mayer 1977; Szpunar 1987; Říhovský 1992; Vankilde 1996, 55). There are two basic forms, with and without the cutting edge slightly expanded to form points, the former possibly resulting from frequent

Figure 4.1 Polished rectangular flint knives from North Dale – Grindale, East Yorks. (courtesy of Martin Green: photo David Cousins).

resharpening and subsequent use as mould prototypes by south-eastern TRB copper-working groups. The type was long-lived but appears to have been circulating in Poland between 3400 and 2900 cal BC (Szpunar 1987, 14 and 17), probably emanating from a Mondsee source. Significantly, Novotná notes that many 'have the appearance of sheet metal' (1970, 18), an additional point of morphological similarity to polished rectangular knives (Figure 4.2).

Seamer axes and Duggleby adzes

Turning to Seamer axes and Duggleby adzes we are again faced with a form that lacks either precedent or functional advantage, yet made huge demands on the flint workers' skill. If this set them apart as prestige objects why was only the blade area polished? And why was this often carried out to a glass-like level? Adze form is also difficult to explain – Chappel (1987, 128) found only 49 definite or probable axe/adzes amongst a sample of 1159 stone axes (4.2%) and most were small implements whose asymmetry could be the unintentional result of resharpening. If such rarity was their attraction this fails to account for the comparable Seamer axe series.

European copper flat axes again furnish close parallels (Figure 4.3). By virtue of casting in one-piece moulds, asymmetric cross sections are not uncommon, particularly amongst Danish trapezoidal axes (Vankilde 1996, fig. 16). Bytyń A axes, the commonest trapezoidal type in Poland, furnish the closest correspondence. They were found alongside rectangular axes in the Kreisrz hoard and are thus considered to date to the same horizon (Szpunar 1987, 14–18). Their distribution centres on the Oder and the Baltic hinterland, extending into Denmark.

Figure 4.2 Continental rectangular copper flat axes with British polished rectangular flint knives – morphology. Row 1 Poland (Mayer 1977, 61, 62, 24, 59, 60); Row 2 Slovakia and Moravia (Novotná 1970, 71a, 70, 69, 67; Říhovský 1992, 133); Row 3 Austria (Szpunar 1987, 181, 173, 180, 175); Row 4 Britain – Aldro C75, Duggleby Howe, Arbor Low, North Dale (2) (Manby 1974, figures 34 and 36; Durden 1995, figure 1).

Against such an equation must be set the limited polishing encountered on Seamer and Duggleby implements and any attempt by the copiers to render the characteristic flat profile and thick butt of the copper flat axe. Could this, however, be explained in terms of the way in which these axes (unlike the rectangular type) were encountered by the Later Neolithic inhabitants of Eastern Yorkshire? If hafted, binding is likely to have covered all but the blade itself – as with the Iceman's axe (Barfield 1994, 14).

If the aim of the Duggleby and Seamer series was to imitate rare, highly valued copper axes this might also explain their almost exclusive production from coastal Devensian till

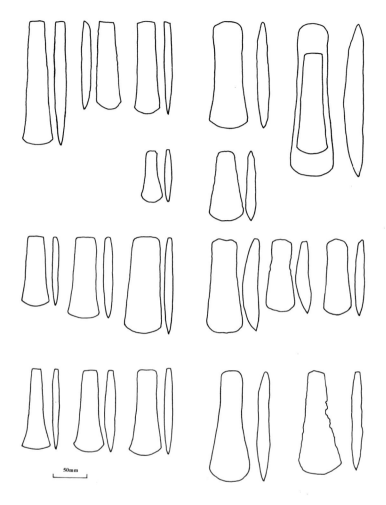

50mm

Figure 4.3 Continental trapezoidal copper flat axes (left) and Seamer – Duggleby flint axes / adzes (right) – morphology. Row 1: S12, M90, S11, York, Duggleby Howe (with P55 imposed); Row 2 P35, Seamer Moor; Row 3 P45, M119, M114, Potter Brampton, Willerby Carr, Biggar, Lanarkshire; Row 4 P6, M86, P44A, Kingston Upon Thames, Harrowgate. [P = Poland (Szpunar 1987); M = Moravia (Říhovský 1992); S = Slovakia (Novotná 1970); flint axes after Manby 1974, figure 42; Kinnes et al. 1983; Ashbee 1970, figure 41; Sheridan 1992, figure 15.4; Adkins and Jackson 1978, 185; Kent 1937.].

flint rather than 'foreign' stone. In addition to its fine flaking properties Manby (1979, 69) notes 'The majority [of these artefacts] were produced in fine quality coloured flints – in red, yellow, orange and mottled varieties' – broadly the colour range of copper.

Jet belt sliders

In view of the common reference to their placement on the hips of skeletons, a role as belt sliders has generally been accepted (McInnes 1968). Nevertheless, in the three cases where this can be attested the evidence suggests they were recovered rather too low for a waist belt: Painsthorpe 118: 'Close to the pelvis, just below the right femur...' (Mortimer 1905, 127); Handley Down 26: '...close to the upper part of the femur...' (Pitt Rivers 1898, 140); and Radley 'resting on his hip' 0.20m below the waist and, perhaps significantly, almost at a right angle to the body, not parallel as might be expected for a belt slider (Bradley 1992,

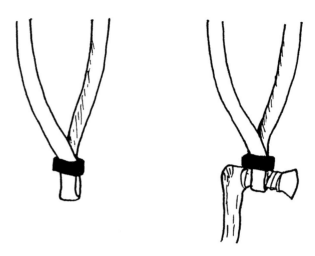

Figure 4.4 Possible use of a jet belt slider as a runner on a baldric.

132 and fig. 5). A prestige role as a copy of a wooden slider for the base of a baldric might be proposed (Figure 4.4) – perhaps the most effective way to carry an axe (*cf.* the parallel alignment of Seamer axe and jet belt slider at Whitegrounds: Brewster 1984, 12). And, if the presence of copper axes is entertained, the pure black of Whitby jet might accord a symbolic contrast, akin to that witnessed later in the Clandon mace head.

Antler maceheads

While hardly justifying the labels 'prestige' or 'elaborate' if judged by indices of technological skill and labour input, the association of maceheads with rich grave inventories demands their inclusion (Kinnes 1979, 65). A symbolic role seems certain since their potential function as axe sleeves is discounted by lack of depth and frequently intact cartilage. Prominence accorded to the bulbous crown in each case may hold the key. Simple axes/ hammers produced in the long, and possibly continuous, tradition of antler and bone working along the eastern littoral of the North Sea and the Baltic (Classon 1983) would, in a worn state, closely resemble British maceheads (Figure 4.5). Only the transitional Mesolithic/Neolithic date of the Staines perforated antler beam mattock hints at the possibility of a southern insular survival of such a tradition (Bonsall and Smith 1990, Table 3). Dates within the 2nd half of the 4th millennium cal BC returned by four antler maceheads from the Thames in London belie this, however, and point to a distinctive Middle Neolithic phenomenon (Loveday *et al.* 2007).

Boars' tusk blades

Boars' tusks are a further exotic addition to the grave repertoire. Their value as a tool need

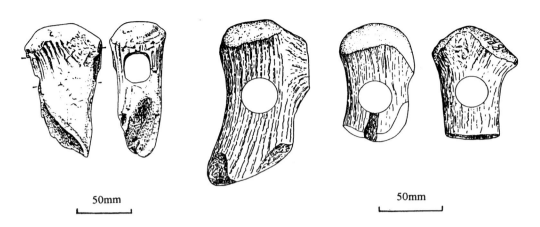

Figure 4.5 Continental antler axes and British antler maceheads. Left to right: Grotte de Han, Belgium (Mariën 1981); Thames, London; Thames, Teddington; Brentford (Simpson 1996, 13, 37, 35).

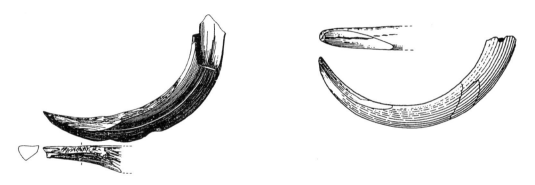

Figure 4.6 Boar tusk blades. Left: Ringkloster (Anderson 1995, figure 21); Right: Duggleby Howe (Kinnes et al. 1983 figure 4, 48).

not be in doubt, as continuity of use testifies (Butler and van der Walls 1966). The presence of 12 boars' tusks and two beaver incisors, variously sliced or abraded, with burial 7 at Duggleby Howe certainly suggests a tool kit (Kinnes *et al.* 1983), yet single and double specimens with a number of other prestige assemblages (*e.g.* Liffs' Low; Ayton East Field) appear to indicate an equally important symbolic role. This may lie in the field of emergent male prestige symbols but it is worth recalling that use of boars' tusks was a feature of Baltic littoral groups from Ertebølle to Pitted Ware (Figure 4.6) (Stenberger 1939; Jażdżeweki 1965, 52; Clark 1975; Anderson 1995, 38–9).

Discussion – context and antecedents

To sum up this brief review of novel 'prestige' artefacts: two types seem best explained as examples of virtuoso craftsmanship in flint stimulated by metal models; two others find partial antecedents on the other side of the North Sea; and one may represent a belt fitting whose status was signalled by its raw material source in Eastern Yorkshire. These conclusions are united by the suggested transportation of copper artefacts beyond the currently proven Danish end of the exchange chain (Randsborg 1979) to reach Britain some 500 years in advance of Beaker metallurgy, most plausibly through the agency of North Sea coastal communities.

The idea that flint axes with expanded blades were produced to emulate metal counterparts is not of course new (Evans 1897, 75), but once their early date had been established it was effectively abandoned. A further problem was seen to be the lack of accurate replication of form, in contrast to Beaker flint daggers (Healey 1984, 16). The hypothesis under consideration here suggests an answer to these difficulties by proposing the movement of a handful of axes at most. In such a circumstance veneration rather than investigation might be predicted, leading to the replication of purely visible features and the magnification of accoutrements (antler 'hammers' and boars' tusks) to a symbolic role. Evidence to support this idea is, with the exception of a trapezoidal flat axe provenanced simply to Norfolk (Needham 1979, 274), no more than circumstantial; this may remain the case, since rarity would have inhibited deposition. That we should not exclude such circumstances is of course the lesson of the 'early' date of the Iceman's axe (Barfield 1994).

Copper artefacts could not move alone, however. Thus if we hypothesise their presence, corroborative evidence might be expected in the form of other artefacts betraying continental origins or affinities. These include a scatter of thick-butted Scandinavian axes (Piggott 1938, 101; Anderson 1984; Holgate 1988, 332–5), and axes of probable Danish marbled flint (Sheridan 1992; Saville 2000), along with polished flint chisels of Vlaardingen type (Manby 1974, 90; Bakker 1979, 86.) Peterborough Ware ceramics, particularly in the Ebbsfleet style, also exhibit certain shared traits with TRB, Pitted Ware and Vlaardingen traditions (Burchell and Piggott 1939, figs 6 and 9). All have a generally eastern distribution but only polished flint chisels are concentrated in Eastern Yorkshire. Since elaborate artefacts have also been recorded in significant numbers from the Thames in London (Adkins and Jackson 1978; Cotton 1984), perhaps it is to this area that we should look for postulated copper artefacts and the origins of replication.

Certainly Ebbsfleet's presence there appears largely riverine and outwith, or secondary to, causewayed enclosures even when the two are not far distant (*e.g.* Thorpe and Staines: Grimes 1960, 405–420; Robertson-Mackay 1987; Springhead and Orsett: Burchell and Piggott 1939; Hedges and Buckley 1978) – a fact which must call into question its role as an Earlier Neolithic regional tradition. Nevertheless comparison of artefact types with those of Eastern Yorkshire, where published lists permit, suggests the latter area numerically dominates in axes (Table 4.1). Only antler maceheads register a strong local presence, perhaps significantly in a potentially mundane context that contrasts with their role as prestige burial accompaniments in northern England.

Equally, Kenworthy (1977; 1981) and Sheridan (1992) both emphasise that uniformity of design, size, quality and coloration all mark out Scottish 'prestige' waisted flint axes as

	1. GREATER LONDON		2. EAST YORKSHIRE
	Dry	Watery	
Concave sided axes	5	7	27
Edge ground axes	1	5	125
Antler maceheads	5	39 (? +1)	2 (?+2)

Table 4.1 Frequency of selected Later Neolithic prestige artefacts in Greater London and Eastern Yorkshire. This data draws on 50 km squares: Greater London (1) Egham to Erith (W–E) and Caterham to Cheshunt (S–N); and Eastern Yorkshire (2) Malton to Flamborough Head (W–E) and Pocklington to Goathland (S–N). Sources: Manby 1974; Holgate 1988; Simpson 1996).

imports from Eastern Yorkshire. Thus there seems little doubt that the genesis of elaborate artefact production can be localised there. Yet short of direct contact across the North Sea (to which polished chisels may alone bear witness), we must explain the attraction of postulated copper prototypes to this area. To do so it is instructive to examine the one feature that sets Eastern Yorkshire apart – the great ritual complex that lies at the bend of the Gypsey Race.

THE RUDSTON COMPLEX

Nature and antecedents

At Rudston the tallest standing stone in Britain by nearly a metre (7.8 m) is boxed in by a unique arrangement of cursus monuments which, despite incomplete recovery, almost equal in combined length the great Dorset complex (Dymond 1966; Stoertz 1997, figs 10 and 11). Yet there are significant differences. The standing stone is an obvious one but more telling is the relationship to long barrows. In Wessex cursus monuments are found amidst their densest concentrations and physically or spatially linked to them; at Rudston the cursus monuments lie in an area where long barrows are all but absent (Kinnes 1992, fig. 1A.20). Here the single secure example (Rudston TA3, *ibid*. 42–43; Stoertz 1997, figs 8 and 10) was ignored by the cursus builders despite lying within a kilometre of the terminals of sites B and C (Figure 4.7). Cropmark long enclosures are concentrated in the area (*ibid*. figs 8 and 9) but few very closely parallel long barrow morphology and they again fail to replicate the Wessex long barrow-cursus spatial relationship. Nor can round barrows be advanced for a comparable role: the claimed Neolithic site of South Side Mount lies 800m away from cursus A while cropmark ring ditches are neither incorporated in the manner of that at Aston on Trent (Gibson and Loveday 1987) nor placed across a terminal.

The inescapable conclusions are that either long barrows were redundant or that the cursus builders were distinct and operating in an area from which long barrow building had been all but excluded (Figure 4.8). The former can now be discounted by the early *terminus ante quem* furnished by a fine ogival arrowhead with Towthorpe affinities recovered from a pit cutting the secondary fill of cursus A, probably from *within* a recut (Abramson 2000).

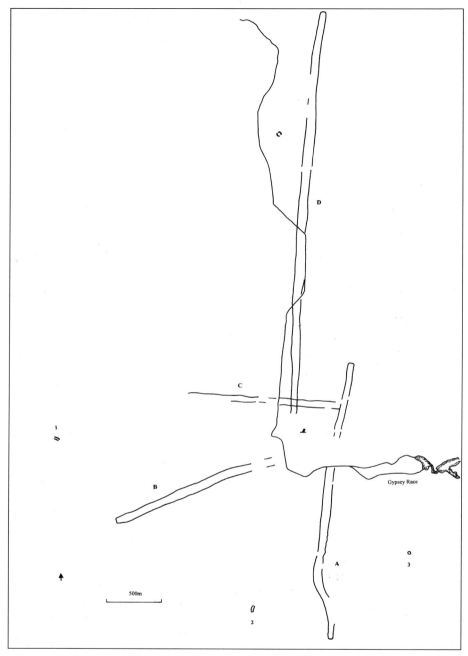

Figure 4.7 The Rudston monolith and cursus complex. A–D = cursuses; 1 = long barrow (Kinnes 1992, TA3), with possible diminutive second site to the south; 2 = possible long enclosure (Stoertz 1997, figure 8, 30); 3 = South Side Mount.

Figure 4.8 Long barrow distribution on the Yorkshire Wolds (dashed line = theoretical Neolithic coastline after Manby 1988, fig. 4.1).

As late clearance also seems precluded by the pollen profile from nearby Willow Garth (Bush and Flenley 1987), the menhir itself attains considerable explanatory significance. The manner in which the cursus monuments surround it strongly implies that it was the primary element of the complex; the alternative requires us to accept the huge stone being dragged across at least one of the cursuses to fill the inexplicably empty central space. Yet the menhir lacks any ready parallel within the causewayed enclosure/long barrow 'package' that characterises the southern British Earlier Neolithic generally (Thomas 1988), or within the round barrow tradition specific to the area (Kinnes 1979; Harding 1997). Raising of substantial posts might, however, have formed an element of West European Mesolithic practice (*cf.* the Stonehenge car park post holes whose dates and species identification leave little room for doubt: Vatcher and Vatcher 1973; Cleal *et al.* 1995, 471–3). If so, the stone at Rudston could stand in direct succession. Such a pre-existing element of the cultural landscape could be predicted to occasion respect and adoption (*cf.* Sundstrom 1996 on the transference of mythologies relating to the Black Hills).

This is heightened by its location at a hydrologically important point, below which the expanded flow of the intermittent Gypsey Race is indicated geographically by its course (Lewin 1969, 51) and historically by medieval records of flooding (Allison 1976, 101). Defoe records in the country near Bridlington: 'at some certain seasons, for none knows when it will happen, several streams of water gush out of the earth with great violence, spouting up a huge heighth, being really natural *jette d' eaus* or fountains; that they make a great noise, …..the country people have a notion that whenever those *gipsies*, or, as some call 'em, *vipseys*, break out, there will certainly ensure either famine or plague' (1724–26 (1927), 246). Multiple springs just to the east of the ritual complex (Bush 1988; Manby pers. comm.) are the most predictable location of dramatically increased flow along the Gypsey Race – an undoubtedly auspicious event, particularly when associated with seasonal revitalisation of the upper course (Abramson 2000). This may have led to their perception as gateways to another world (*cf.* Elaide 1954; Bradley 2000). Perhaps, significantly, they also fed a now vanished estuary beyond Bridlington (Figure 4.8) of very considerable potential to Mesolithic communities whose presence is recorded beside the river (Manby 1973).

Whether or not its antecedents were Mesolithic, demarcation of the Rudston location by a gigantic stone must have ensured more than local impact. And, that like the Grand Menhir at Lochmariquer, the shape of the stone resembled an axe may not have been overlooked (Bradley 1990, 55; Edmonds 1995, 53). An abiding problem in the study of Later Neolithic Eastern Yorkshire is the density of Group VI axes. Since neither superior mechanical properties (Bradley and Edmonds 1993) nor selection for prestige waisted forms (Manby 1979, 69–70) explain this concentration, mythological ones might. In wet conditions the Gypsey Race migrates westwards up the Great Wold Valley, appearing as a 'gypsey' near Wold Newton and again near Duggleby, and this was the general direction of the Lake District Massif. (*cf.* Silverman 1994, 8 on the mythologised source of the spring at Cahuachi).

Cult sites and individual power

Powerful male and female elements may well have been perceived in the conjunction of monolith and springs at Rudston, conceivably elevated to that union of sky and earth so familiar from creation myths. Such cult sites have the capacity to draw material, as well as a transient population, from a distance vastly in excess of the 25 to 30 km radii of chiefdoms (Spencer 1990, 7; Renfrew 1993, 9). With no visible reciprocal commodity to explain the striking Group VI axe concentration in Eastern Yorkshire, a religiously sanctioned tribute relationship might be conceived. The presence of Group I and VII axes, and such an exotic item as a carved stone ball in the Eastern Wolds (Manby 1974, 100), all at the extremities of their distribution, confirms drawing power well beyond that of a simple chiefdom.

Such a cult site model, however, appears to leave unresolved the question of elite burial since Thorpe and Richards (1984) equate ritual control with the opposite – a suppression of individuality within great monument building projects. Nevertheless the two are by no means mutually exclusive. Mississippian mounds leave little doubt that ritual was central to that society, yet rich interments and the production of speciality artefacts point to social ranking from an early stage (Steponaitis 1991, fig. 9.3). Likewise the Andean Early Horizon Chavin phenomenon was followed by the appearance of a small number of rich burials. Since these possessed objects decorated with Chavin iconographic devices it is suggested that a symbolic link was being made between leadership and divine sanction. Spread of the ideology to other centres, through it is argued the medium of pilgrimage, may have been encouraged by regional leaders eager to circumvent earlier, local egalitarian ideologies and so legitimate their appropriation of wealth (Burger 1995, 203–7). In each case elites emerged through identification *with*, or control *of*, the cult site – *not* in opposition to it. Significance must surely, therefore, be accorded to the evidence, slight as it is, that construction of the Rudston complex preceded the advent of 'prestige' individual burial but that the defining artefact types are concentrated in its vicinity.

CONCLUSIONS

Analysis of the problems posed by the primary evidence from Eastern Yorkshire suggests that the Rudston complex can be cast as a cult site of inter-regional significance, with antecedents outwith Earlier Neolithic causewayed enclosure/long barrow orthodoxy, and that the elaborate artefacts can be conceived as either copies of copper originals or of their accoutrements. These notions are united by the presumption that the former acted as an engine drawing artefacts such as the latter to it. Thus an historically specific conjunction of two long distance networks – one operating along the eastern littoral of the North Sea (Louwe Kooijmans 1987), and possibly extended to the Lower Thames or East Anglia by creek exploiting groups, and the other a ritual field conceivably drawing material and groups to the Rudston complex through centres such as Maxey and Fornham All Saints – may have transformed local Later Neolithic society. Movement of other artefacts along the eastern coastline is well attested (Edmonds 1995, 104). Once they had crossed the threshold of the North Sea the impact of copper artefacts would undoubtedly have been heightened but still dependent on the internal characteristics of local traditions (Helms 1988; Sorensen 1989, 199; Bradley and Edmonds 1993, 15): muted perhaps amongst ostensibly egalitarian groups in Southern England; magnified in Eastern Yorkshire where parallel communities placed contrasting emphasis on the individual and the communal through burial practices (Harding 1997). If one lineage held a monopoly of certain forms of ritual power at the cult site (a familiar ethnographic and historic feature), such '...gifts...from an other world of spirits and gods...' (Whittle 1996, 120) may have been deployed to confirm divine sanction for the adoption of ranking.

Such a catalyst is of course akin to that which may trigger a prestige goods system, a model put aside at the outset of this discussion. Nevertheless it should be recalled that a continued flow of the prized items through long distance trade is central to such a social development (Friedman and Rowlands 1977) not simply a short impact phase of the sort hypothesised here. An inter-regional cult model by contrast not only furnishes an explanation for the presence in East Yorkshire of the proposed prototypes, it also suggests a restricted sphere within which prestige flint copies may have acted as 'tokens of identity' (Edmonds 1998) – that of the lineage claiming proprietary rights. If simple edge polished axes moved amongst lower lineages a context can be offered to the observation that, '... distinctions within and between groups were mediated through... portable items ...whose distinctive form and material...may have been important in fixing their association with certain ideas, and perhaps with certain kinds of social relationship' (Bradley and Edmonds 1993, 205–6). Equally it suggests a possible resolution to the problem posed by the national correlation of Group VI axe dispersal with the adoption of individual burial, yet their exclusion from the rite (*ibid.*). As emblematic elements embodying ideas specific to the cult site prior to the arrival of copper prototypes, their public sphere may have been restricted to the ceremonial (*cf.* the axe located in a pit at the centre of the Maxey cursus: Simpson 1985, 249), while acting as a conduit for ideas of individual power.

It may not be insignificant that southwards from the Thames valley, where Group VI axes were to be replaced by Group I as the dominant type (*ibid.*), cursus builders adopted the regionally distinctive strategy of incorporating (and perhaps nullifying) existing long barrows/enclosures in bank and ditch lines. Interpretation of this practice in evolutionary terms has long encouraged the notion of a southern origin for cursus monuments, yet in a model of expansive cult development, incorporation of earlier monuments defines distance *from* the centre rather than proximity *to* it. Since Wessex alone possesses a cursus complex comparable to Rudston in scale (Barrett *et al.* 1991), the possibility could be entertained that a challenge is being witnessed here – a familiar feature of the cult phenomenon as distant elites break away from primary site dominance (*cf.* Cresswell 1958, 17). While the considerable distance separating the Yorkshire Wolds and Wessex 'core areas' suggests caution, the potential role of intermediate centres such as Dorchester upon Thames in articulating the spread of ideas should not be dismissed (Loveday 1999). Thus, if ideologically driven, as with the Chavin phenomenon (Burger 1995), developments in one region may have triggered those in others. The encoding role of artefacts in this process was critical since, as with Mississippian chiefdoms, it seems likely that these '…special wealth objects were often associated with powers that both symbolised and encapsulated the elites' divinity or at least non local legitimacy' (Earle 1991, 7). The uniquely complex pattern of burials in the great mound raised at Duggleby, near the uppermost spring of the Gypsey Race, may record that point in the Neolithic of Eastern Yorkshire at which an existing ideology was usurped to legitimate individual wealth and power (Loveday 2002).

A date of 4597±35 BP (OxA – 13327) (3500–3130 cal. BC) has been obtained from the antler macehead accompanying the central upper burial (G) that was also associated with a lozenge arrowhead and a Duggleby-type flint adze (Loveday *et al* 2007). Along with the phase 2 burial at Whitegrounds, some 10km away, that was accompanied by a jet belt slider and a Seamer-type axe and dated 4520±90 BP (HAR5507) (3350–3030 cal BC), this points to the introduction of at least five types of elaborate artefact in the second half of the 4th millennium cal. BC. Determinations from seven other sampled antler maceheads (with one exception) correspond with this (3500–2900 cal. BC), as do dates from Peterborough Ware (Gibson and Kinnes 1997) and most English cursuses; Scottish sites have returned earlier dates (Loveday 2006; Thomas 2006). A Middle Neolithic transformation is indicated that spans much of southern Britain and antedates the Grooved Ware-henge phenomenon of Wessex. Its peculiar intensity in East Yorkshire, where elaborate artefact production and accompanied individual burial appear to have been initiated, is best explained as a regional response to historically specific circumstances that, fuelled by ritual, was to have far wider repercussions.

ACKNOWLEDGEMENTS

I am very grateful to Terry Manby, Alex Gibson, Mike Parker Pearson, Stuart Needham and Richard Bradley for reading and commenting upon this paper. They are not of course implicated in its conclusions. Particular thanks go to Martin Green for starting this train of thought by showing me his superb examples of polished rectangular knives, and to David Cousins for photographing them.

Bibliography

Allison, K. J., 1976, *The Making of the English Landscape. The East Riding of Yorkshire*. London. Hodder and Stoughton.

Anderson, J. N., 1984, *Scandinavian–type Thick Butted Flint Axes in Britain: a Comparative Study*. Unpublished dissertation. University of Reading.

Anderson, S. H., 1995, Ringkloster. Ertebølle trappers and wild boar hunters in eastern Jutland. A survey. *Journal of Danish Archaeology*, 12, 13–59.

Abramson, P., 2000, Excavations at Pits Plantation, Rudston, for Perenco UK Ltd. *East Riding Archaeologist*, 10, 1–22.

Adkins, R. and Jackson, R., 1978, *Neolithic Stone and Flint Axes from the River Thames* (British Museum Occasional Paper I). London. British Museum.

Bakker, J. A., 1979, *TRB West Group. Studies in the Chronology and Geography of the Makers of Hunebeds and Tiefstich Pottery*. Amsterdam. Amsterdam University Press.

Barfield, L., 1994, The Iceman reviewed. *Antiquity*, 68, 10–26.

Barrett, J., Bradley, R. and Green, M., 1991, *Landscape, Monuments and Society. The prehistory of Cranborne Chase*. Cambridge. Cambridge University Press.

Bonsall, C. and Smith, C., 1990, Bone and Antler Technology in the British Late Upper Palaeolthic and Mesolithic: The Impact of Accelerator Dating. In P. Vermeersch and P. van Peer (eds), *Contributions to the Mesolithic of Europe. Papers presented at the Fourth International Symposium 'The Mesolithic in Europe', Leuven 1990*. Leuven. Leuven University Press. 359–368.

Bradley, R., 1990, *The Passage of Arms: An Archaeological Analysis of Prehistoric Hoards and Votive Deposits*. Cambridge. Cambridge University Press.

Bradley, R., 1992, The excavation of an oval barrow beside the Abingdon causewayed enclosure, Oxfordshire. *Proceedings of the Prehistoric Society*, 58, 127–42.

Bradley, R., 2000, *An Archaeology of Natural Places*. London. Routledge.

Bradley, R. and Edmonds, M., 1993, *Interpreting the Axe Trade: Production and Exchange in Neolithic Britain*. Cambridge. Cambridge University Press.

Brewster, T. C. M., 1984, *The Excavation of Whitegrounds Barrow 1, Burythorpe, North Yorkshire*. Malton. East Riding Research Committee Publications.

Burchell, J. P. T. and Piggott, S., 1939, Decorated Prehistoric Pottery from the bed of the Ebbsfleet, Northfleet, Kent, *Antiquaries Journal*, 19, 405–420.

Burger, R. L., 1995, *Chavin and the origin of Andean Civilisation*. London. Thames and Hudson.

Bush, M. B., 1988, Early Mesolithic Disturbance: A Force in the Landscape. *Journal of Archaeological Sciences*, 15, 453–462.

Bush, M. B. and Flenley, J. R., 1987, The age of the British chalk grassland. *Nature*, 329, 434–436.

Butler, J. J. and van der Waals, J. D., 1966, Bell beakers and early metal working in the Netherlands. *Palaeohistoria*, 12, 41–139.

Chappell, S., 1987, *Stone Axe Morphology and Distribution in Neolithic Britain* (BAR British Series 177). Oxford. British Archaeological Reports.

Clark, J. G. D., 1928, Discoidal polished flint knives, their typology and distribution. *Proceedings of the Prehistoric Society of East Anglia*, 6, 41–54.

Clark, J. G. D., 1975, *The Earliest Stone Age Settlement of Scandinavia*. Cambridge. Cambridge University Press.

Clarke, D. V., Cowie, T. G. and Foxon, A., 1985, *Symbols of Power at the Time of Stonehenge*. Edinburgh. HMSO.

Classon, A., 1983, Spoolde. *Palaeohistoria*, 25, 77–130.

Cleal, R. M. J., Walker, K. E. and Montague, R., 1995, *Stonehenge in its landscape. Twentieth century excavations* (English Heritage Archaeological Report 10). London. English Heritage.

Cotton, J., 1984, Three later Neolithic discoidal knives from NE Surrey: with a note on similar examples from the county. *Surrey Archaeological Collections*, 75, 225–33.

Cresswell, K. A. C., 1958, *A Short Account of Early Islamic Architecture*. Harmondsworth. Penguin.

Defoe, D., 1927, *A Tour Through England and Wales II*. London. Everyman, Dutton.

Durden, T., 1995, The production of specialised flintwork in the later Neolithic: a case study from the Yorkshire Wolds. *Proceedings of the Prehistoric Society*, 61, 409–432.

Dymond, D. P., 1966, Ritual monuments at Rudston, East Yorkshire. *Proceedings of the Prehistoric Society*, 32, 86–95.

Earle, T., 1991 The evolution of chiefdoms. In T. Earle (ed.), *Chiefdoms: Power, Economy and Ideology*. A School of American Research Book. Cambridge: Cambridge University Press. 1–15.

Earnshaw, J. R., 1995, *A Neolithic Flint Industry Site at Grindale, near Bridlington*. Bulletin of the Prehistoric Research Section: Yorkshire Archaeological Society, 32.

Edmonds, M., 1995, *Stone Tools and Society. Working Stone in Neolithic and Bronze Age Britain*. London. Batsford.

Edmonds, M., 1998, Sermons in Stone: Identity, Value, and Stone Tools in Later Neolithic Britain. In M. Edmonds and C. Richards (eds), *Understanding the Neolithic of North Western Europe*. Glasgow. Cruithne Press. 248–276.

Elaide, M., 1954, *The Myth of the Eternal Return*. London. Arkana.

Evans, J., 1897, *The ancient Stone Implements, Weapons and Ornaments of Great Britain*. London.

Friedman, J. and Rowlands, M. J., 1977, Notes towards an epigenetic model of the evolution of "civilisation". In J. Friedman and M. J. Rowlands (eds), *The Evolution of Social Systems*. London. Duckworth. 210–276.

Gibson, A. and Kinnes, I., 1997, On the urns of a dilemma: radiocarbon and the Peterborough problem. *Oxford Journal of Archaeology*, 16 (1), 65–72.

Gibson, A. and Loveday., R, 1989, Excavations at the cursus monument of Aston on Trent. In A. Gibson (ed.), *Midlands Prehistory. Some recent and current researches into the prehistory of central England* (BAR British Series 204). Oxford: British Archaeological Reports. 27–50.

Grimes, W. F., 1960, *Excavations on Defence Sites 1939–1945 1. Mainly Neolithic and Bronze Age*. London: HMSO.

Harding, J., 1997, Interpreting the Neolithic: The Monuments of North Yorkshire. *Oxford Journal of Archaeology*, 16, 279–295.

Healey, E., 1984, The Flint Axe. In T. C. M. Brewster, *The Excavation of Whitegrounds Barrow 1, Burythorpe, North Yorkshire*. Malton: East Riding Archaeological Research Committee Publications. 15–17.

Hedges, J. D. and Buckley, D. G., 1978, Excavations at a Neolithic causewayed enclosure, Orsett, Essex, 1975. *Proceedings of the Prehistoric Society*, 44, 219–308.

Helms, M., 1988, *Ulysees' Sail*. Princeton: Princeton University Press.

Holgate, R., 1988, *Neolithic Settlement of the Thames Basin* (BAR British Series 194). Oxford: British Archaeological Reports.

Jażdżewski, K., 1965, *Ancient Peoples and Places: Poland*. London. Thames and Hudson.

Kenworthy, J. B., 1977, A Reconsideration of the 'Ardiffery' finds, Cruden, Aberdeenshire. *Proceedings of the Society of Antiquaries of Scotland*, 108, 80–93.

Kenworthy, J. B., 1981, The flint adze blade and its cultural context. In J. N. G. Ritchie and H. C. Adamson. Knappers, Dunbartonshire: a reassessment, *Proceedings of the Society of Antiquaries of Scotland*, 111, 172–204.

Kinnes, I., 1979, *Round barrows and Ring ditches in the British Neolithic* (British Museum Occasional Paper 7). London. British Museum.

Kinnes, I., 1992, *Non-megalithic long barrows and allied structures in the British Neolithic* (British Museum Occasional Paper 52). London. British Museum.

Kinnes, I., Schadla-Hall, T., Chadwick, P. and Dean, P., 1983, Duggleby Howe Reconsidered. *Archaeological Journal*, 140, 83–108.

Lewin, J., 1969, *The Yorkshire Wolds. A Study in Geomorphology* (Occasional Papers in Geography No. 11). Hull. University of Hull.

Lewis, B., 1987, *The Martin Green Collection of lithic artefacts from North Dale, parish of Grindale, Humberside*. Unpublished manuscripts, Martin Green Collection, Down Farm, Woodcutts, Dorset.

Louwe Kooijmans, L. P., 1987, Neolithic settlement and subsistence in the Wetlands of the Rhine/Meuse Delta of the Netherlands. In J. Coles and A. J. Lawson (eds), *European Wetlands in Prehistory*. Oxford. Clarendon Press. 227–251.

Loveday, R., 1999, Dorchester-on-Thames – Ritual Complex or Ritual Landscape? In A. Barclay and J. Harding (eds), *Pathways and ceremonies. The cursus monuments of Britain and Ireland* (Neolithic Studies Group Seminar Papers 4). Oxford. Oxbow. 49–66.

Loveday, R., 2002, Duggleby Howe Revisited. *Oxford Journal of Archaeology*, 21, 135–146.

Loveday, R., 2006, *Inscribed Across the Landscape: the Cursus Enigma*. Stroud. Tempus.

Loveday, R., Gibson, A., Marshall, P. D., Bayliss, A., Bronk Ramsey, C. and van der Plicht, H., 2007, The Antler Macehead Dating Project. *Proceedings of the Prehistoric Society*, 73, 381–92.

Manby, T. G., 1973, The Finds. In J. R. Earnshaw, The Site of a Medieval Post Mill and Prehistoric Site at Bridlington. *Yorkshire Archaeological Journal*, 45, 19–40.

Manby, T. G., 1974, *Grooved Ware sites in Yorkshire and the North of England* (BAR British Series 4). Oxford. British Archaeological Reports.

Manby, T. G., 1975 Neolithic occupation sites on the Yorkshire Wolds. *Yorkshire Archaeological Journal*, 48, 23–60.

Manby, T. G., 1979 Typology, materials and distribution of flint and stone axes in Yorkshire. In T. H. McK Clough and W. A. Cummins (eds), *Stone Axe Studies: volume 1* (CBA Research Report 23). London. Council for British Archaeology. 65–81.

Manby, T. G., 1988, *Archaeology in Eastern Yorkshire. Essays in Honour of T. C. M. Brewster*. Sheffield. Sheffield University Department of Archaeology and Prehistory.

McInnes, I., 1968, Jet Sliders in Late Neolithic Britain. In J. M. Coles and D. D. A. Simpson (eds), *Studies in Ancient Europe: Essays presented to Stuart Piggott*. Leicester. Leicester University Press. 137–144.

Mariën, M., 1981, Cuillères en os type Han-sur-Lesse (Néolithique S.O.M.). *Helinium*, XXI, 1–20.

Mayer, E. F., 1977, Die Äxte und Beile in Österreich. *Prähistorische Bronzefunde Abteilung*, IX, 9. Munchen. Beck'sche Verlagsbuchhandlung.

Mortimer, J. R., 1905, *Forty Years Research in British and Saxon Burial Mounds in Eastern Yorkshire*. London.

Needham, S., 1979, The extent of foreign influence on Early Bronze Age development in Southern Britain. In M. Ryan (ed.), 265–293.

Novotná, M., 1970 Die Äxte und Beile in der Slowakei. *Prähistorische Bronzefunde Abteilung*, IX, 3. Munchen. Beck'sche Verlagsbuchhandlung.

Pierpoint, S., 1980, *Social Patterns in Yorkshire Prehistory* (BAR British Series 74). Oxford. British Archaeological Reports.

Piggott, S., 1938, The Early Bronze Age in Wessex. *Proceedings of the Prehistoric Society*, 4, 52–106.

Pitt-Rivers, A. H. L. F., 1898, *Excavations in Cranborne Chase IV*. Privately printed.

Pitts, M., 1996, The Stone Axe in Neolithic Britain. *Proceedings of the Prehistoric Society*, 62, 311–372.

Radley, J. and Cooper, B., 1968 A Neolithic Site at Elton: an experiment in field recording. *Derbyshire Archaeological Journal*, 88, 37–46.

Randsborg, K., 1979, Resource, Distribution and the Function of Copper in Early Neolithic Denmark. In M. Ryan (ed.), 303–318.

Renfrew, C., 1993, Trade beyond the Material. In C. Scarre and F. Healy (eds), *Trade and exchange in Prehistoric Europe*. Oxford. Oxbow. 5–16.

Říhovský, J., 1992, Die Äxte, Beile, Meisel und Hämmer in Mähren. *Prähistorische Bronzefunde Abteilung*, IX, 17. Stuttgart. Franz Steiner Verlag.

Robertson-Mackay, R., 1987, The Neolithic causewayed enclosure at Staines, Surrey: excavations 1961–3. *Proceedings of the Prehistoric Society*, 53, 23–128.

Ryan, M., (ed.) 1979, *The Origins of Metallurgy in Atlantic Europe. Proceedings of the 5th Atlantic Colloquium*. Dublin. Stationery Office.

Saville, A., 2000, Axehead Information Requested, *Past*, 34, 11–12.

Sheridan, A., 1992, Scottish stone axeheads: some new work and recent discoveries. In N. Sharples and A. Sheridan (eds), *Vessels for the Ancestors. Essays on the Neolithic of Britain and Ireland. Edinburgh*. Edinburgh University Press. 194– 212.

Silverman, H., 1994, The archaeological identification of an ancient Peruvian pilgrimage center. *World Archaeology*, 26.1, 1–18.

Simpson, D. D. A., 1996, 'Crown' Antler Maceheads and the Later Neolithic in Britain. *Proceedings of the Prehistoric Society*, 62, 293–310.

Simpson, W. G., 1985, Excavations at Maxey, Bardyke Fields, 1962–63. In F. Pryor and C. French (eds), *The Fenland Project No. 1. Archaeology and Environment in the Lower Welland Valley Volume 2* (East Anglian Archaeology 27). Cambridge. Cambridge Archaeological Committee. 245–264.

Sorensen, M. L., 1989, Ignoring innovation, denying change. In R. Torrence and S. van der Leeuw (eds), *What's new? A closer look at the process of innovation*. London. Unwin Hyman. 182–202.

Spencer, C. S., 1990, On the Tempo and Mode of State Formation: Neoevolutionism reconsidered. *Journal of Anthropological Archaeology*, 9, 1–30.

Steponaitis, V., 1991, Contrasting patterns of Mississippian development. In T. Earle (ed.), *Chiefdoms: Power, Economy and Ideology. A School of American Research Book*. Cambridge. Cambridge University Press. 193–228.

Stoertz, C., 1997, *Ancient Landscapes of the Yorkshire Wolds. Aerial photographic transcription and analysis*. London. Royal Commission on Historical Monuments (England).

Stenberger, M., 1939, Das Västerbjersfeld: Ein Grabfeld der Ganggräberzeit auf Gotland. *Acta Archaeologica*, 10, 60–105.

Sundstrom, L., 1996, Mirror of heaven: cross cultural transference of the sacred geography of the Black Hills. *World Archaeology*, 28.2, 177–189.

Szpunar, A., 1987, Die Beile in Polen I (Flachbeile, Randleistenbeile, Randeistenmeisel). *Prähistorische Bronzefunde Abteilung* IX, 16. Munchen: Beck'sche Verlagbuchhandlung.

Thorpe, I. J. and Richards, C., 1984, The Decline of Ritual Authority and the introduction of Beakers into Britain. In R. Bradley and J. Gardiner (eds), *Neolithic Studies. A Review of Some Current Research* (BAR British Series 133). Oxford. British Archaeological Reports. 67–84.

Thomas, J., 1988, Neolithic explanations revisited: the Mesolithic-Neolithic transition in Britain and south Scandinavia. *Proceedings of the Prehistoric Society*, 54, 59–66.

Thomas, J., 2006, On the origins and development of cursus monuments in Britain. *Proceedings of the Prehistoric Society*, 72, 229–241.

Vandkilde, H., 1996, *From Stone to Bronze. The metalwork of the Late Neolithic and Early Bronze Age in Denmark*. Aarhus. Jutland Archaeological Society Publications.

Vatcher, F. de M. and Vatcher, H. L., 1973, Excavation of three postholes in Stonehenge carpark, *Wiltshire Archaeology and Natural History Magazine*, 68, 57–63.

Whittle, A., 1996, *Europe in the Neolithic. The Creation of New Worlds*. Cambridge. Cambridge University Press.

Chapter 5

Building monuments at the centre of the world: exploring regional diversity in south-west Wales and south-west Scotland

Vicki Cummings

INTRODUCTION

Today south-west Wales and south-west Scotland are relatively difficult to access, with low population densities and are often considered peripheral areas of Britain. However, in the Neolithic this situation may have been rather different. In this paper it is suggested that these two areas were at the very centre of a Neolithic world that had its focus around the Irish Sea. Within this broader area it is possible to identify regional differences, both between and within areas, which were manifested in the landscape setting and the form of the chambered monuments. In particular, the significance of the landscape in defining distinctive regions will be addressed. However, there are also relationships between the monuments and landscape features that suggest that people may have conceived of themselves as part of a much wider community that spanned the Irish Sea area as a whole.

REGIONS IN SOUTH-WEST WALES

South-west Wales and south-west Scotland have dense concentrations of chambered monuments and are part of a broader distribution of megaliths found all along the coasts of the Irish Sea. I will begin by focussing on the chambered monuments of south-west Wales. There are 28 sites in this area that incorporates Pembrokeshire and western Carmarthenshire. There is a dense distribution of sites in northern Pembrokeshire with a few additional outliers to the south and west. South-west Wales is bounded to the north, west and south by the sea, and there is a 'blank' area with no monuments to the east. There has been considerable debate regarding the classification of the chambered tombs of south-west Wales (Grimes 1936; Daniel 1950; Lynch 1972, 1976; Barker 1992) as they do not seem to fit neatly into easily recognised typological groups. Furthermore, the monuments of south-west Wales are not morphologically identical to sites found elsewhere in the Irish Sea zone, making their exact origins hard to pinpoint. However, I have suggested that it is possible to divide the sites in this area into two main forms of monument (Cummings 2001, 2002a; Cummings and Whittle 2004). First, there are the sites that draw their inspiration from portal dolmens and simple passage graves found all along the Irish Sea coasts. These sites consist of a megalithic chamber defined by a large bulky capstone set on top of several uprights (Figure 5.1). This includes cairns such as Pentre Ifan which was set within a long

Figure 5.1 The dolmens of Petre Ifan (top left) and Carreg Samson (top right), and the earth-fast sites of Carn Wnda (bottom left) and Coetan Arthur (bottom right).

cairn (Grimes 1948), and sites like Carreg Samson which would have had a small passage leading to the chamber (Lynch 1975). The second type of monument in south-west Wales has been described as 'earth-fast' (Daniel 1950) and these sites were constructed using a small thin capstone propped up at one end (Figure 5.1). Both these monument forms are found throughout south-west Wales, and from architecture alone it is not easy to define any distinctive regions within this area (see Figure 5.5). Architecturally, these two forms of monument are in marked contrast to the Cotswold-Severn chambered tombs found further east (from the Gower to the Black Mountains) that suggests that a regionally distinctive and discrete form of monument construction existed in south-west Wales.

The monuments of south-west Wales also share a number of characteristics in their overall landscape setting which again contrasts with monuments found further east (Cummings and Whittle 2004). Many megaliths across south-west Wales are positioned in the vicinity of rocky outcrops, and these outcrops either appear to be skylined on the horizon as at Pentre Ifan (Figure 5.1; Tilley 1994, 106) or as part of the site itself, as at Carn Wnda (Figure 5.1; Cummings 2002a). Almost all sites have views of the sea and also of mountains (Fowler and Cummings 2003), such as the crag of Carn Llidi to the west or Carn Ingli and the Preseli Mountains to the east. All monuments are set on a gentle slope or up against outcrops and this restricts the view in one direction (Cummings 2001). The ways in which monuments were used may also have created broader connections across this area but unfortunately very little material culture has been recovered from these sites and it is therefore only possible to speculate on this point at present. Other similarities

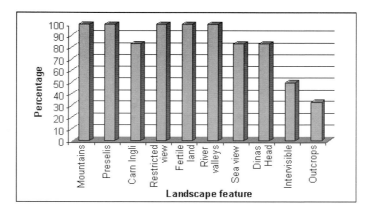

Figure 5.2 The landscape setting of the Nevern Group of monuments in south-west Wales.

may have been manifested in forms of material culture such as pottery and polished stone axes in this region: for example Group VIII axes from northern Pembrokeshire are found throughout south-west Wales (Clough and Cummins 1988).

Broadly speaking, then, there are similarities in the architecture and landscape settings of the monuments of south-west Wales. This suggests that this area may have been a distinctive region in the Neolithic. A closer examination of the landscape settings of these sites also enables us to suggest that there may have been smaller, more localised regions *within* south-west Wales in the Neolithic. The first of these regions centres around the Nevern Valley and Frances Lynch (1972) has already discussed the significance of this area in the Neolithic. Architecturally, there are notable differences between the monuments (see Barker 1992), yet they are all set within remarkably similar landscape settings (Figure 5.2). All have views of the Preselis, all are set on fertile land and all are positioned along river valleys. The vast majority of sites have views of Carn Ingli (Tilley 1994, 105), a view of the sea and a view of Dinas Head. In this area, however, vicinity to outcrops is not as significant as in other areas. Half of the sites are also intervisible.

Assertions of the significance of the landscape in relation to these monuments have recently been criticised by Fleming (1999, 121) who argues that it would be hard to position a monument in this area without a view of features such as Carn Ingli. However, one monument in this area does just that and this is the site of Bedd yr Afanc (Figure 5.3). This site is located in a radically different landscape setting from the other chambered monuments in the area. In fact, its location in open moorland with wide-ranging views in all directions is almost identical to that of the stone circle at Gors Fawr 6km to the south (Figure 5.3). On its own this is not enough to suggest that this monument should be considered as separate from the chambered monuments, but it is also structurally unique. Consisting of two small rows of stone, this site remains unparalleled in Wales. It has been interpreted as a gallery grave (see Grimes 1936, 1939), which, taken with its locational similarities with stone circles, may suggest it was a late import to the region. This site also demonstrates that landscape setting was a critical component of each site, and that some

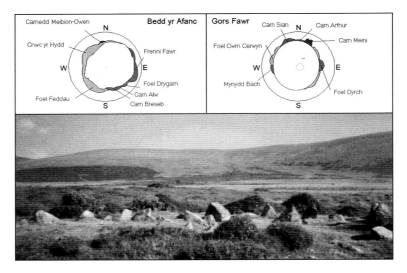

Figure 5.3 Top: schematic landscape settings of Bedd yr Afanc and Gors Fawr stone circle. Below: the Bedd yr Afanc monument, set in a similar location to Gors Fawr.

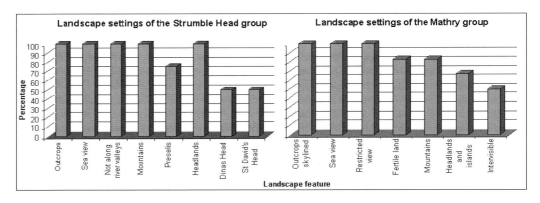

Figure 5.4 The landscape settings of the Strumble Head and Mathyr groups.

sites were carefully positioned not to have views of features such as Carn Ingli and the sea. This reinforces the suggestion that the other monuments were carefully positioned in order to have views of features like Carn Ingli.

Through a close examination of landscape setting, it is possible to identify several other discrete groupings in south-west Wales. The group of four earth-fast monuments on Strumble Head are all located in remarkably similar locations as well as being structurally alike. All sites are located close to or directly up against outcrops with wide views of the sea, headlands and the mountains (Figure 5.4). Another regional group is found around Mathry. This group consists of six structurally similar monuments set in very similar

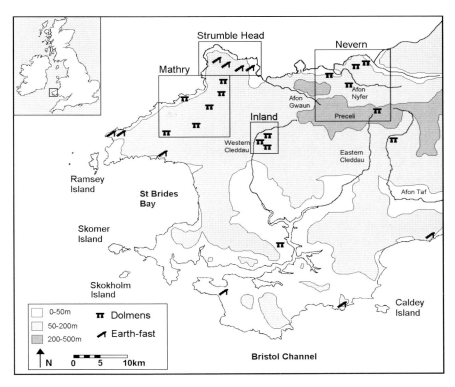

Figure 5.5 The regional groupings within south-west Wales.

landscape settings in a spatially discrete part of western Pembrokeshire (Figure 5.4). All sites are built so that outcrops are skylined on the horizon, and all have a view of the sea, even sites such as Treffynnon that is over 5km from the coast. Another group is a set of three monuments located in inland Pembrokeshire. Therefore it is possible to suggest that even though there are some broader similarities between monuments in south-west Wales, there may also have been several smaller regional groupings that were defined through monumental architecture and landscape setting (Figure 5.5).

REGIONS IN SOUTH-WEST SCOTLAND

South-west Scotland has a rather different set of monuments. For the purposes of this paper, south-west Scotland consists of Dumfries and Galloway and southern Ayrshire and has a total of 29 monuments with 'blank' areas to the north and east, and the Irish Sea to the west and south. The classification of monuments in this area has been detailed by Henshall (1972) with minor alterations by Murray (1992) and Cummings (2002b). As with south-west Wales, there is a dense concentration of monuments, in this case in the

Figure 5.6 The Clyde monuments of Cairnholy I (top left) and Mid Gleniron (bottom left) and the Bargrennan sites of Bargrennan (top right) and Cairnderry (bottom right). Plans after Henshall 1972.

west of Galloway, with a spread of outliers throughout the rest of the area. Like south-west Wales, there are also two main types of monument. There are some Clyde monuments in south-west Scotland which are found throughout western Scotland as a whole (see Henshall 1972; and Scott 1969). The Clyde monuments of south-west Scotland are structurally quite different in their initial phases, consisting of small simple chambers surrounded by sub-rectangular cairns (as at Mid Gleniron: Corcoran 1969). However in their later phases these sites become more homogeneous, with the addition of megalithic façades and long cairns (Figure 5.6). In contrast, the Bargrennan monuments consist of small chamber or chambers that are set within round cairns (Henshall 1972; Murray 1992). These monuments would appear to be single-phase, although few sites have been excavated, and the date of these sites also remains contested: late Neolithic pottery was found at the White Cairn, Bargrennan but on the paving of the passage (Piggott and Powell 1949); more recently excavations at Cairnderry and Bargennan White Cairn were conducted with the hope of dating the construction of these monuments, but no dateable material was found (for the construction phase, Cumings and Fowler 2002). There has also been considerable debate regarding the origins of these two different monument forms. The Clyde monuments have been considered part of what was once the 'Clyde-Carlingford' culture, with clear connections being suggested between the Galloway monuments and the court cairns of north-east Ireland (Childe 1940; Piggott 1954).

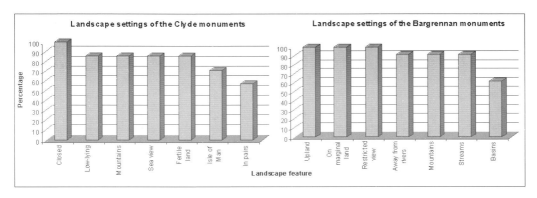

Figure 5.7 The landscape settings of the Clyde and Bargrennan monuments.

It is also possible to define several distinctive regional groups within south-west Scotland. These groups are defined by the structural components of the chambered monuments and are reinforced by their landscape settings. The Clyde monuments are found along the south-west coast of Galloway and all of these monuments are located in similar places in the landscape, in low-lying areas on fertile land with views of mountains and the sea (Figure 5.7). Four of the monuments are located in pairs and over two-thirds of sites have wider views out over the Isle of Man (for more details see Cummings 2002b). In contrast, the Bargrennan group is not only structurally quite different to the Clyde monuments but is also located in entirely different landscape settings. These sites are positioned in upland basins, away from the river valleys with views over the Merrick mountains (Cummings 2002b). This spatially discrete group of monuments with its shared landscape settings would seem to suggest that this area may have been another region within the broader area of south-west Scotland in the Neolithic. Other spatially discrete group of monuments can be identified such as the two long cairns of Slewcairn and Lochhill in eastern Dumfries and Galloway. These sites were built from wood in their first phases (Masters 1973; Kinnes 1992) and are also positioned in quite different settings from their western counterparts. This seems to suggest that Neolithic south-west Scotland may have been divided not only between the upland and lowlands, but also between the east and west where different monument traditions reinforced by different landscape settings marked out distinct areas (Figure 5.8).

DISCUSSION

I have suggested that it is possible to define distinctive regions by examining the landscape settings and the structural remains of monuments. However, I would like to emphasise that this does not imply that these areas were bounded or fixed throughout the Neolithic. These distinctions may mark out boundaries of only one sphere of life, perhaps reinforcing differences between localised belief systems. Other forms of material culture may have emphasised other regional boundaries or identities as well as connections across broader

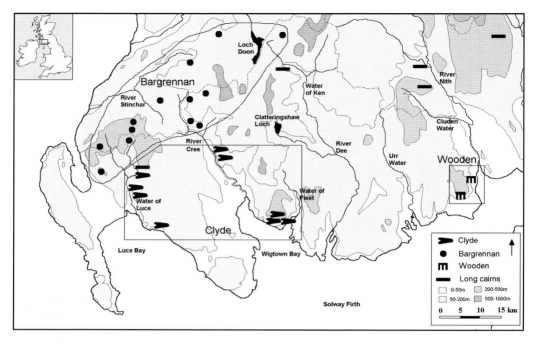

Figure 5.8 The regional groupings within south-west Scotland.

areas. Different monuments set within distinctive regions in an area like south-west Wales or south-west Scotland may indicate areas of the landscape that were used for different purposes, relating to both the living and the dead. Some areas may have been used seasonally, perhaps for the movement of livestock (this can be suggested for the upland Bargrennan monuments: Cummings 2002b). Other areas may have been considered places appropriate only for the dead. Regional distinctions may also indicate a *temporal* division of the landscape. This may be particularly relevant in the case of south-west Scotland where it is possible to suggest that the Bargrennan monuments may have been built at a later date than the Clyde monuments, marking out the use of different parts of the landscape over time (and see discussion in Cummings and Fowler 2007). Therefore, regional differences expressed in monumental form may reflect the use of these localised regions through a seasonal or yearly round.

Although it is possible to define a series of distinctive regions within both south-west Wales and south-west Scotland there were also broader themes in the landscape setting of monuments which suggests there may have been ties *across* the Irish Sea area. Connections across the Irish Sea have been sought for many years in the actual architecture of the monuments. For example, in south-west Wales it has been suggested that Bedd yr Afanc has Irish origins (Grimes 1936, 128) and Cerrig y Gof has been paralleled with Mull Hill on the Isle of Man (Lynch 1972, 81; Darvill 2000, 376). The portal dolmens have also been likened to monuments in Ireland (Lynch 1972). In north Wales it has been suggested that the passage graves of Bryn Celli Ddu and Barclodiad y Gawres originate in Ireland

(Daniel and Powell 1949; Powell and Daniel 1956; Lynch 1967), as do the façades found on the Clyde monuments in south-west Scotland and at Pentre Ifan (Lynch 1972, 71). We have already noted that the Clyde monuments of south-west Scotland have been linked to court cairns in Ireland (*e.g.* de Valera 1960) and the Bargrennan monuments have also been paralleled with Irish passage graves (Murray 1992, 39). Some of these architectural comparisons are problematic but the movement of material culture such as polished stone axes within the Irish Sea zone does support the idea that there were connections between these areas (Sheridan 1986, 2000; Saville 1994, 1999; Cooney 2000, 226).

The suggestion that there were broad connections across the Irish Sea zone can be reinforced by a consideration of the landscape settings of the monuments. In south-west Wales and south-west Scotland as well as north-west Wales, monuments seem to have been located to have views of quite specific landscape features. In all three of these areas monuments are set on the upper reaches of low-lying fertile land with wide views of the sea and of mountains (Cummings and Whittle 2004). Monuments in all areas are positioned on the sides of hills so that they would have been skylined when approached and so that there is a restricted view in one direction. Thus a person encountering a chambered monument in south-west Scotland would see landscape features similar to those seen by a person encountering a chambered monument in north-west or south-west Wales (Cummings 2003). This is not the case with other monuments in these regions such as stone circles which are positioned in quite different landscape settings from the chambered monuments (see Figure 5.3).

What was important may not simply have been which landscape features were visible from each monument. Instead, it may have been *what could be seen from the places that the monuments referenced*. For example, it has already been shown how the monuments of the Nevern Valley seem to be carefully positioned so that there are clear views of Carn Ingli. We could explain this relationship by suggesting that Carn Ingli was a significant and symbolic local feature that was tied into local myth and legends. However, while this may well have been the case, there may have been other reasons for the significance of this particular landscape feature. Standing on the summit of Carn Ingli it is possible to see all of the other important landscape features that are visible from the chambered monuments throughout south-west Wales. From the summit of Carn Ingli there are clear views of the Preselis to the east, Carn Llidi to the west, and Stumble and Dinas Head to the north. These are the major landscape features that are visible from the chambered monuments in the area, and it seems as if Carn Ingli sits at the very *centre* of this landscape. It is particularly relevant that from the Preselis, only a few kilometres away from Carn Ingli, all of these landscape features are not visible simultaneously. The importance of Carn Ingli, therefore, may not have been that it was visible from a number of the chambered monuments, *but that all of the significant places in south-west Wales were visible from its summit*. In this sense, Carn Ingli sits at the centre of the world in south-west Wales, and this may explain why many chambered monuments have views of this feature.

It has also been noted that many sites in the Nevern Valley have views of the Preselis, in particular Carn Meini. Other sites in south-west Wales also have views of the Preselis and Carn Meini including Carreg Samson over 22km away to the west and the Devil's Quoit 37km to the south-west. Carn Meini may have been significant for a number of reasons including the presence of an axe factory (Clough and Cummins 1988) and the fact that the natural outcrops which cover the summit look as though they have been built by people

(Bradley 2000, 95; Cummings 2002a). But the Preselis may also have been significant because they had views of other key places in the Irish Sea zone, namely Snowdonia in north Wales and the Wicklow Hills in Ireland to the west (Miles 2001; Cummings 2004).

A similar situation is found elsewhere along the eastern side of the Irish Sea. Landscape features which are repeatedly visible from monuments or which have a monument close by have views of distant places. In north Wales, the Preselis, Cumbria, the Isle of Man and Ireland are visible from many locations. For example, the site of Lletty'r Filiast stands on the side of Great Ormes Head from which the Isle of Man and Cumbria are visible. From different points in the Snowdon range, which is visible from most sites in north Wales, key landscape features around all parts of the Irish Sea are visible including Ireland, the Preselis and even the Merrick mountains and Criffel in south-west Scotland (Jesty 2000). In fact, a number of the monuments in north Wales have direct views of these distant places. For example, it is possible to see the Preseli mountains from a number of the monuments on the Lleyn Peninsula and beyond, including Dyffryn Ardudwy. Furthermore, from the monument of Barclodiad y Gawres it is possible to see Ireland over 70km distant (Powell and Daniel 1956). Likewise in Dumfries & Galloway many of the Clyde monuments have views out to the Isle of Man. Most of the Bargrennan monuments have clear views of the Merrick Mountains from which it is possible to see Snowdonia and Ireland. Even the wooden mortuary structures to the east of south-west Scotland are set around the mountain of Criffel from which it is possible to see Cumbria, Snowdonia and Ireland. In this way, each monument in the Irish Sea zone seems to have been carefully located in relation to features that have views over other parts of the Irish Sea zone, visually connecting all the different regions (Bowen 1970). This may have enabled people to feel part of wider Neolithic community that spanned the entire Irish Sea area. This in turn may have been crucial in understanding the very origins of monumentality and a Neolithic way of life (see Cummings 2004 for the full argument regarding intervisibility across the Irish Sea).

CONCLUSION

It has been suggested that an examination of the structural remains, in combination with the landscape settings of monuments, means that it is possible to identify a number of spatially discrete regions within south-west Wales and south-west Scotland. In both these areas, which in terms of the monuments may themselves have been broader regions within the Neolithic, smaller areas have been identified. These regional differences may relate to how sites were used in different parts of the landscape or to areas associated with different groups of people. However, there were also shared features at monuments found in both these regions and across the Irish Sea zone as a whole. It seems that monuments were positioned at specific points in the landscape while also creating connections between more distant places. In particular it has been suggested that the landscape features visible from the monuments were part of a broader network of interconnected places which referenced one another and which bound together all parts of the Irish Sea zone. Although the monuments created smaller local areas within regions which may have been linked to a localised mythological understanding of the world, the intervisibility of the Irish Sea zone itself may have enabled people to feel part of a broader Neolithic community. Thus, south-west Wales and south-west Scotland may be on the periphery today, but in the Neolithic they may have been part of a broader world which spanned the Irish Sea. Therefore, people in these areas were literally building monuments at the very centre of their world.

ACKNOWLEDGEMENTS

This research was conducted as part of a doctoral thesis, and I would like to thank the School of History and Archaeology, Cardiff University for funding my Ph.D. Subsequent research was undertaken as part of the 'Megaliths in the Neolithic landscapes of Wales' project, and I would like to thank the Board of Celtic Studies for funding this research. Many thanks to Chris Fowler and Alasdair Whittle for comments on earlier drafts of this paper and to Robert Johnston for help with issues of intervisibility.

Bibliography

Barker, C., 1992, *The chambered tombs of south-west Wales: a reassessment of the Neolithi burial monuments of Carmarthenshire and Pembrokeshire.* Oxford. Oxbow.

Bowen, E. G., 1970, Britain and the British Seas. In D. Moore (ed.), *The Irish Sea province in archaeology and history.* Cardiff. Cambrian Archaeological Association. 13–28

Bradley, R., 2000, *The archaeology of natural places.* London. Routledge.

Childe, V. G., 1940, *Prehistoric communities of the British Isles.* Edinburgh. Edinburgh University Press.

Clough, T. and Cummins, W., (eds), 1988, *Stone axe studies: volume two.* London. Council for British Archaeology.

Cooney, G., 2000, *Landscapes of Neolithic Ireland.* London. Routledge.

Corcoran, J., 1969, Excavation of two chambered cairns at Mid Gleniron Farm, Glenluce Wigtownshire. *Transactions of the Dumfries and Galloway Natural History and Antiquarian Society*, 46, 31–90.

Cummings, V., 2001, *Landscapes in transition? Exploring the origins of monumentality in south-west Wales and south-west Scotland.* Unpublished Ph.D. Thesis. Cardiff University.

Cummings, V., 2002a, All cultural things: actual and conceptual monuments in the Neolithic of western Britain. In C. Scarre (ed.), *Monumentality and landscape in Atlantic Europe.* London. Routledge. 107–121.

Cummings, V., 2002b, Between mountains and sea: a reconsideration of the Neolithic monuments of south-west Scotland. *Proceedings of the Prehistoric Society*, 68, 125–46.

Cummings, V., 2003, Building from memory: remembering the past at Neolithic monuments in western Britain. In H. Williams (ed.), *Archaeologies of remembrance: death and memory in past societies.* London: Klewer Plenum. 25–44.

Cummings, V., 2004, Connecting the mountains and sea: the monuments of the eastern Irish Sea zone. In V. Cummings and C. Fowler (eds), *The Neolithic of the Irish Sea: materiality and traditions of practice.* Oxford: Oxbow. 29–36.

Cummings, V. and Fowler, C., 2007, *From cairn to cemetery: an archaeological investigation of the chambered cairns and early Bronze Age mortuary deposits at Cairnderry and Bargrennan White Cairn, south-west Scotland.* Oxford: BAR.

Cummings, V. and Whittle, A., 2004, *Places of special virtue: Megaliths in the Neolithic landscapes of Wales.* Oxford. Oxbow.

Daniel, G., 1950, *The prehistoric chamber tombs of England and Wales.* Cambridge. Cambridge University Press.

Daniel, G. E. and Powell, T. G. E., 1949, The distribution and date of the passage-graves of the British Isles. *Proceedings of the Prehistoric Society*, 14, 169–187.

Darvill, T., 2000, Neolithic Mann in context. In A. Ritchie (ed.), *Neolithic Orkney in its European context*. Oxford. Oxbow. 371–385.

de Valera, R., 1960, The court cairns of Ireland. *Proceedings of the Royal Irish Academy*, 60, 9–140.

Fleming, A., 1999, Phenomenology and the megaliths of Wales: a dreaming too far? *Oxford Journal of Archaeology*, 18, 119–125.

Fowler, C. and Cummings, V., 2003, Places of transformation: building monuments from water and stone in the Neolithic of the Irish Sea. *Journal of the Royal Anthropological Institute*, 9, 1–20.

Grimes, W., 1936, The megalithic monuments of Wales. *Proceedings of the Prehistoric Society*, 2, 106–139.

Grimes, W., 1939, Bedd y Afanc. *Proceedings of the Prehistoric Society*, 5, 258.

Grimes, W., 1948, Pentre Ifan burial chamber, Pembrokeshire. *Archaeologia Cambrensis*, 100, 3–23.

Henshall, A., 1972, *The chambered tombs of Scotland, volume two*. Edinburgh. Edinburgh University Press.

Jesty, C., 2000, *A guide to the view from the summit of Snowdon*. Bridport: Jesty's Panoramas.

Kinnes, I., 1992, Balnagowan and after: the context of non-megalithic mortuary sites in Scotland. In N. Sharples and A. Sheridan (eds), 83–103.

Lynch, F., 1967, Barclodiad y Gawres. *Archaeologia Cambrensis*, 116, 1–22.

Lynch, F., 1972, Portal dolmens in the Nevern Valley, Pembrokeshire. In F. Lynch and C. Burgess (eds), *Prehistoric man in Wales and the west*. Bath. Adams and Dart. 67–84.

Lynch, F., 1975, Excavations at Carreg Samson megalithic tomb, Mathry, Pembrokeshire. *Archaeologia Cambrensis*, 124, 15–35.

Lynch, F., 1976, Towards a chronology of megalithic tombs in Wales. In G. Boon and J. Lewis (eds), *Welsh antiquity: essays mainly on prehistoric topics presented to H. Savory*. Cardiff. National Museum of Wales. 63–79.

Masters, L., 1973, The Lochhill long cairn. *Antiquity*, 47, 96–100.

Miles, D., 2001, The Presely Hills. *Rural Wales*, 2001, 14–15.

Murray, J., 1992, The Bargrennan group of chambered cairns: circumstance and context. In N. Sharples and A. Sheridan (eds), *Vessels for the Ancestors*. Edinburgh: Edinburgh University Press. 33–48.

Piggott, S., 1954, *The Neolithic cultures of the British Isles*. Cambridge. Cambridge University Press.

Piggott, S. and Powell, T., 1949, The excavation of three Neolithic chambered tombs in Galloway. *Proceedings of the Society of Antiquaries of Scotland*, 83, 103–161.

Powell, T. G. E. and Daniel, G. E., 1956, *Barclodiad y Gawres: the excavation of a megalithic chamber tomb in Anglesey 1952–1953*. Liverpool. Liverpool University Press.

Saville, A., 1994, Exploitation of lithic resources for stone tools in earlier prehistoric Scotland. In N. Ashton and A. David (eds), *Stories in stone*. London. Lithic Studies Society. 57–70.

Saville, A., 1999, A cache of flint axeheads and other flint artefacts from Auchenhoan, near Campbeltown, Kintyre, Scotland. *Proceedings of the Prehistoric Society*, 65, 83–123.

Scott, J., 1969, The Clyde cairns of Scotland. In T. G. E. Powell, J. X. W. P. Corcoran, F. Lynch, and J. Scott (eds), *Megalithic enquiries in the west of Britain*. Liverpool. Liverpool University Press. 175–222.

Sharples, N. and Sheridan, A., (eds), *Vessels for the ancestors: essays on the Neolithic of Britain and Ireland*. Edinburgh. Edinburgh University Press.

Sheridan, J. A., 1986, Porcellanite artefacts: a new survey. *Ulster Journal of Archaeology*, 49, 19–32.

Sheridan, A., 2000, Achnacreebeag and its French connections: vive the 'Auld Alliance'. In J. Henderson (ed.), *The prehistory and early history of Atlantic Europe*. Oxford: BAR International Series 861. 1–15.

Tilley, C., 1994, *A phenomenology of landscape*. Oxford. Berg.

Chapter 6

On the edge of England: Cumbria as a Neolithic region

Aaron Watson and Richard Bradley

INTRODUCTION

In a recent paper, Ewan Campbell asked the question 'were the Scots Irish?' (Campbell 2001). He was considering the distinctive region of early medieval Scotland known as Dalriada, the capital of which was Dunadd, close to Kilmartin. He suggested that one way of perceiving social relations across the Irish Sea was to think in terms of a political unit that extended from Ireland into Argyll. It was united by the sea, and separated from the rest of Scotland by the Highland mountains. This is a reminder that regionality in the past need not have followed modern political boundaries. In this paper, we would like to suggest that a similar relationship once existed in the Neolithic between Cumbria, on the edge of England, and the east of Ireland.

CUMBRIA IN CONTEXT

Like Dalriada, Cumbria is geographically distinct. The Irish Sea constitutes its western margin, while the Pennine Hills bound the east. Within this region are the Lake District mountains, surrounded by a coastal plain and the Vale of Eden (Figure 6.1). Both of these low-lying areas were centres for occupation and monument building in the Neolithic, including long cairns, probable causewayed enclosures, stone circles and at least two henges (Masters 1984; Waterhouse 1985; Soffe and Clare 1988; Topping 1992). The Vale of Eden in particular was a major focus for rock art (Beckensall 1999, 2002), while the central uplands of the Lake District were some of the most productive sources of ground stone axes in the British Isles (Bradley and Edmonds 1993).

In the Neolithic, Cumbria was one of a number of important regions around the Irish Sea. Other notable concentrations of monuments are located in north Wales, south-west Scotland, the Isle of Man, and eastern Ireland. Stone axes quarried in the Lake District were circulated widely throughout these areas, and many were deposited in specialised contexts in Ireland; it has been claimed that their characteristic forms might have been imitated by axeheads there (*ibid.* 1993, 163–4). The chronology of this process remains uncertain, however, and it is equally possible that circumstances in Ireland may have influenced Britain. It is this possibility that the paper aims to explore.

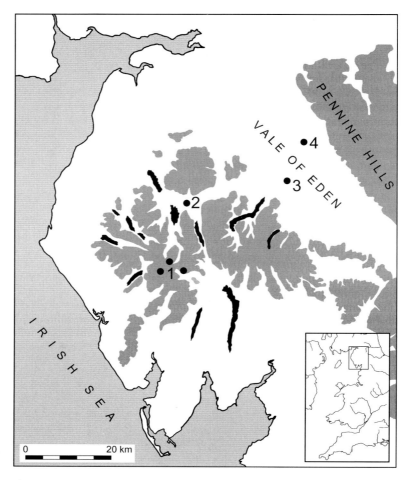

Figure 6.1 The topography of Cumbria including sites mentioned in the text: 1) Stone axe sources in the central Lake District, including Great Langdale; 2) Castlerigg; 3) Mayburgh; 4) Long Meg and Her Daughters. Land above 300m is shown in grey.

IMAGES OF IRELAND

Rock art in Cumbria is most distinctive. A cluster of sites in the Vale of Eden contrast both with rock art elsewhere in Cumbria and across neighbouring regions of northern England and Scotland. Most of the rock art sites in Mid Argyll, Dumfries and Galloway, Northumberland and Yorkshire were carved into near-horizontal outcrops of rock. Art in the Vale of Eden is found upon boulders that are not attached to the bedrock and where the decorated surfaces are steeply sloping or vertical. Also unique in this area of northern Britain are complex spirals carved into standing monuments. At the stone circle of Long Meg and Her Daughters, for instance, a tall outlying monolith has a complex panel of imagery that includes spirals. Nearby, two interconnected spirals are incised into a stone at the probable kerb cairn of Little Meg.

While the location and format of these Cumbrian rock art sites is highly unusual in northern Britain, they would not be out of place in some regions of Ireland. In the Boyne Valley, Co. Meath, rock art that includes complex spirals was incorporated into the fabric of monuments, especially the kerbstones of passage graves like Knowth or Newgrange (O'Kelly 1982; Eogan 1986). A link with passage graves might help to explain the inclusion of chevron decoration at Glassonby in the Vale of Eden, as this design has an extremely limited distribution outside Irish passage grave art. In addition, unusual spirals within the cairn of Old Parks at Kirkoswald in the Vale of Eden have parallels at the Millin Bay megalithic tomb in Ulster (Ferguson 1895; Collins and Waterman 1955).

Overall, it seems that rock art in the Vale of Eden displays characteristics that have rather more in common with sites in the Boyne Valley than northern Britain. In both Cumbria and Ireland, spirals are rare outside monumental contexts and have more in common with the decoration of Irish passage graves than they do with styles of open-air rock elsewhere in Britain. The placement of these images upon steeply inclining surfaces also parallels Irish sites (Bradley 1999). Indeed, their nearest parallels to the east of the Irish Sea are found at the passage graves of Barclodiad y Gawres and Bryn Celli Ddu in Anglesey (Beckensall 1999), monuments whose origin can also be traced to the Irish passage grave tradition.

MAYBURGH: THE AMBIGUITY OF ENCLOSURE

Alongside rock art, the architecture of some Cumbrian monuments also seems indicative of connections to Ireland. While it has long been noted that Cumbrian stone circles like Castlerigg and Swinside share features with the ring at Ballynoe in County Down (Burl 1976, 58–9, 238), we would like to consider Mayburgh, a large embanked enclosure in the Vale of Eden. This site would not be out of place among later Neolithic enclosures in the Boyne Valley (Topping 1992, 262–3). Like those monuments, the banks at Mayburgh appear to have been gathered by hollowing out its interior (Bradley 1998a, 128). The site is often classified as a henge, but its setting and appearance are in marked contrast with henges elsewhere, including the lower-lying King Arthur's Round Table nearby. In combination with the similarities to sites in Ireland, this could suggest that it was early in the sequence of those monuments. King Arthur's Round Table is visible from within Mayburgh, being aligned with the entrance, and it is quite possible that the smaller henge was a later construction located to facilitate this relationship.

With reference to the affinities between Cumbrian and Irish sites, we would like to suggest that the form of Mayburgh was influenced in diverse ways by its distant heritage across the sea.

Mayburgh is understood as an enclosure because it is so often conceived in plan, a perspective that was not available to people in the Neolithic. Indeed, we would have an entirely different impression of the site if we had never been permitted to explore its innermost spaces. Being situated upon a raised glacial mound that overlooks a floodplain, it is very difficult to determine the nature of Mayburgh's morphology from outside its boundaries, and observers in the surrounding landscape can only imagine what its precise format might be.

Figure 6.2 Views towards the exterior of Mayburgh. The house in the lower image provides a sense of scale.

In Cumbria, where henge monuments are rare, it is even possible to mistake Mayburgh for an enormous circular mound (Figure 6.2). The high banks and raised situation of Mayburgh appears uncannily similar to the weathered remains of a large passage grave of a kind that can only be found in the Boyne Valley. The construction of Mayburgh's banks from cobbles even reproduces the cairn material of those monuments, and the single entrance opens to the east, reflecting the passage orientation of many Irish tombs.

Mayburgh challenges archaeological classification because the appearance of the site changes so dramatically when it is experienced in its landscape context. For an audience outside its boundaries, Mayburgh resembles an impenetrable Boyne valley passage grave, but those inside engage with an entirely different place that has closer affinities to the enclosures that post-dated those monuments. Perhaps the act of approaching and entering Mayburgh played out ideas about its history and origins, or maybe ambiguity was itself important. At Ballynahatty in Ulster, a pre-existing passage grave was actually encircled by the Giant's Ring, a large boulder-built enclosure (Collins 1957; Hartwell 1998). Not only did the groundplan of this enclosure itself approximate that of passage graves, with a flattened arc on its eastern side, but the situation of the stone setting with respect to this boundary reproduced the location of a chamber within a large passage grave (Figure 6.3). Perhaps the central surviving stone within Mayburgh, which antiquarian reports suggest was once part of a rather unusual arrangement (Topping 1992, 250–1), might itself have recalled orthostats from a distant and possibly mythicised memory of passage grave chambers.

While acknowledging these parallels, both Mayburgh and the Giant's Ring were not passage graves, and could not have been used like those monuments. We would suggest, however, that elements of the older passage graves might have been reflected in the form of the enclosures that succeeded them. Such developments might have their origins in the sequence identified at passage graves across Britain where activities seem to have become increasingly externalised towards the end of their use (Bradley 1998a, Chapter 7). For example, Newgrange was succeeded by a timber enclosure of similar size that was constructed alongside the mound (O'Kelly 1982). In addition, references to pre-existing architectural forms would not be unprecedented in the Neolithic. Megalithic 'coves' might reproduce the chamber architecture of earlier chambered tombs (Burl 1988), while the Early Bronze Age Clava passage graves in northern Scotland were themselves the reinvention of an ancient architectural tradition (Bradley 2000a, 224).

So far we have suggested that Cumbrian rock art and Mayburgh had a common frame of reference in Ireland. We would now like to consider how such influences might be reflected by stone circles and their close relationships to the wider landscape.

ENCIRCLED SPACES

The large Cumbrian stone circles created an entirely different experience to Mayburgh. These sites consist of permeable arrangements of standing stones rather than continuous perimeters, enabling a quite different relationship between their users and the wider landscape. Two stone circles to the north-east of the Lake District, Castlerigg and Long Meg and Her Daughters, share similar landscape settings. They are situated on low hills where breaks of slope obscure surrounding valleys, creating both a sense of isolation and emphasising elevated horizons of hills. Castlerigg is located in the Vale of Keswick where it is contained by the impressive mountains of the northern Lake District, while Long Meg and Her Daughters has views to the fells of the Lake District, the Yorkshire Dales and the Pennine Hills (Figure 6.4). These settings are typical of stone circles across the British Isles, emphasising a sense of centrality within a landscape that appears to encircle

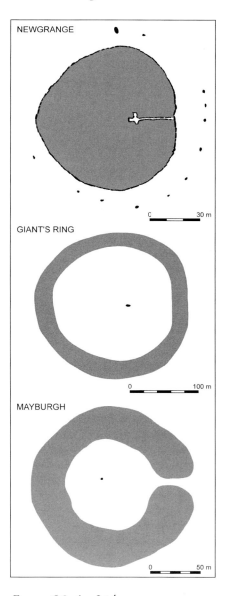

Figure 6.3 An Irish passage grave, an Irish enclosure and Mayburgh shown in plan. Note the similar locations of central features within these monuments. Stones are shown in black, and cairn/rubble material in grey. Plans after O'Kelly (1982), Hartwell (1998) and Topping (1992) respectively.

Figure 6.4 Views from two Cumbrian stone circles. The upper image emphasises the arc of mountains which surround Castlerigg, while distant views of the Lake District are framed by stones and an outlying monolith at Long Meg and Her Daughters.

the monument (Richards 1996; Bradley 1998a, Chapter 8; Watson 2000, 2001a). While the format of stone circles might seem far removed from the mounds of passage graves or the banks of Mayburgh, Long Meg and Her Daughters does feature an outlying monolith decorated with spiral motifs which have their closest parallels in Irish passage grave art.

Boyne Valley passage graves and Cumbrian stone circles are both defined by near-circular boundaries: kerbs and rings of standing stones. These boundaries seem to have operated in quite different ways, however. Passage grave kerbs face *outwards*, so that an audience has to engage with the margins of seemingly impenetrable mounds which, by the later Neolithic, were infrequently accessed or even permanently closed. It is upon these kerbstones that curvilinear motifs proliferate. In contrast, stone circle boundaries can be viewed from both outside and inside, with the spiral images at Long Meg and Her Daughters facing *inwards* so that they could only have been seen by an audience looking out from this monument towards the encircling hills and mountains (Figure 7.5). Rather than relating to an enclosed cairn, these stones and images were intended to be seen in association with the uplands. Not only were standing stones and rock art motifs set against the landscape itself, but the meanings they conveyed might feasibly have extended to that topography as well. Might this suggest a connection between images that have associations with the boundaries of passage graves and the juxtaposition of monuments and landscape in Cumbria?

We will consider these possibilities with reference to other areas in northern Britain that seem to have been treated in special ways. First we will consider the relationships between rock art and distinct geological features, then extend our argument to encompass entire landscapes.

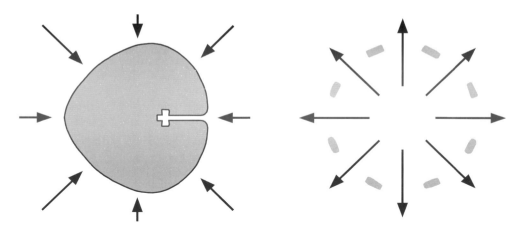

Figure 6.5 The contrasting experience of passage graves and stone circles. An audience can look towards the kerbs of passage graves or be confined within their chambers, while stone circles enable wide views of the surrounding landscape.

READING THE LANDSCAPE

In northern Britain, unusual motifs were sometimes used to distinguish natural places. For instance, confined river gorges such as Morwick in Northumberland or Ballochmyle in south-west Scotland (Beckensall 1999) were decorated with designs that contrast with those in the surrounding landscape. Rather like some of the rock art in the Vale of Eden, not only were these images incised onto vertical surfaces, but they include motifs that would ordinarily only be found at Irish passage graves, including rosettes and spirals. Another case is Roughting Linn in Northumberland, where a large rock outcrop has a frieze of curvilinear imagery deeply incised around its perimeter. The bold nature of these images is quite unlike art in the surrounding landscape, but again invites comparison with the megalithic art more often associated with the kerbs of Irish passage graves (Bradley 1997, 105–7). This referencing of buildings might be very revealing as these natural features arguably reproduce qualities of passage grave architecture, with ravines resembling passageways, and the outcrop at Roughting Linn echoing the profile of passage grave mounds (Bradley 1997, 132).

Rock art not only created connections between specific topographic features and Irish monuments, but also extended these schemes to include wider movement through the world. Across northern England and Scotland there is evidence to suggest that interfaces between distinct topographic zones were also treated in special ways. For instance, the margins of the Milfield basin in Northumberland were demarcated by a series of elaborate rock art panels that emphasised a threshold between two different kinds of landscape, upland and lowland. Comparable patterns have been recognised in the North York Moors, the Kilmartin Valley and Dumfries and Galloway (Bradley 1997, Chapter 6). In some cases, especially elaborate imagery was located at key topographic thresholds along routes that approached major monument complexes such as the Milfield basin or Kilmartin. These were placed to be read by people moving through the landscape, structuring their engagement with pathways and viewpoints, valleys and basins. The landscape itself was being inscribed with information, orchestrating and controlling participants' experiences as if they were negotiating a formal monument. Indeed, the land was being decorated according to a symbolic scheme that might have had its ultimate origins in defining the perimeters and entrances of Irish passage graves (Bradley 1997, 124).

Having outlined instances where landscapes appear to have been interpreted using passage grave architecture as a point of reference, the cluster of monuments with Irish affinities in the Vale of Eden may begin to make more sense. Whether at the passage graves in Ireland, Roughting Linn, or broader landscapes of northern England and Scotland, curvilinear imagery seems to have formalised boundaries and thresholds. In all of these instances, people encountered circles at a variety of different scales, whether individual rock art motifs, the plan of monuments, or transitional points in the wider topography.

We will now turn to the possibility that some significant sites in Cumbria might have distinguished an important contrast between the lowlands and the mountains of the Lake District. This possibility is especially interesting given suggestions that Cumbrian stone circles were situated on routes between the upland sources of stone axes and polishing sites in the surrounding lowlands (Burl 1976, 69). Perhaps these circular monuments in some way mediated and facilitated the passage of people and stone axes between contrasting landscapes.

STONES AND THE SKY

To the west of the Vale of Eden, the Lake District mountains rise to meet the sky (Figure 6.6). This is a major topographic threshold, with the interior of the Lake District creating an entirely different sense of place from the lowlands where people lived. The craggy and largely treeless topography of the high ground visibly contrasts with the subtle contours of the valleys and coastal plain, while the changeable climate, drifting cloud, and shifting light create a sense of liminality and proximity to the sky (Figure 6.7). Ethnographic studies suggest that distinctive places or atmospheric phenomena can be invested with special meanings or mythologies, and mountainous terrain across the world is often perceived as a place apart (Tuan 1977; Taçon 1991; Bloch 1995).

Figure 6.6 A major topographic threshold; the Lake District mountains rise from the Vale of Eden.

Figure 6.7 Stone axes and the sky; cloud and stone meet at the Scafell Pike axe sources in the upper image, while, in the lower, shadows cross the Langdale Pikes.

It was from this extraordinary environment that stone axes were procured, with the major sources being situated around the summits of some of the highest and most impressive mountains; Scafell Pike, Glaramara and the Langdale Pikes (Claris and Quartemaine 1989). Indeed, the choice of extraction sites appears to reflect a preference for spectacular or dangerous locations (Bradley and Edmonds 1993; Watson 1995). In part this may have enabled access to these quarries to be controlled (Bradley and Edmonds 1993, 143), but it could also suggest that certain qualities of the terrain might have been invested with potent and significant meanings. As pieces of these places (Bradley 2000b, Chapter 6) stone axes seem to have been imbued with social value and significance, which could help to explain why they were so often carried to distant destinations across the British Isles.

We suggest that people moving from the Vale of Eden into the Lake District mountains understood this transition in ways which we might ordinarily equate with the division of space at passage graves. If the Vale of Eden acted as a kind of gateway which formalised access to the Lake District and the stone axe quarries, this need not be unlike the fundamental structure of monuments which combined boundaries, entrances and liminal interiors which may not have been accessible to all. We suggest that this distinctive terrain might itself have been perceived in ways that we would ordinarily equate with built architecture, and that such relationships might not be entirely unprecedented. We have already noted that landforms in other parts of northern Britain were treated as if they were architectural, and in these instances the buildings that they referenced could only have been found across the Irish Sea.

DISCUSSION

Overall, we suggest that later Neolithic perceptions of monuments and landscape in Cumbria might have articulated memories of distant places. Rock art in the Vale of Eden recalls styles of decoration that are almost unknown outside Irish passage grave art. Mayburgh was inspired not only by enclosures in Ireland, but also appears to reproduce characteristics of the enormous mounds that preceded them in the Boyne Valley. Through these transformations, ideologies and cosmologies that had formerly been restricted to the interiors of monumental buildings in Ireland seem to have been expanded to accommodate a larger audience. This process had its origins at the mounds themselves, but we suggest that in the later Neolithic it extended to both monuments and landscapes across the Irish Sea. Stone circles seem to reflect the most extreme extension of these symbols. Rather than being contained within a mound, an audience could occupy the interior of these circles and look out into the world (Figure 6.5). In many ways, these sites turned the concept of the passage grave inside out, extending their meanings to open monuments and wider landscapes (Watson 2000). Long Meg and Her Daughters juxtaposed the landscape against potent and meaningful rock art motifs that had previously possessed exclusive associations with passage graves. Just as the treatment of natural features and landscapes elsewhere in northern Britain seems to have referenced Ireland, perhaps perceptions of the Cumbrian landscape might also have been empowered through similar memories.

In the Neolithic, entering passage graves like those in the Boyne Valley is likely to have been a profound and dynamic event. These monuments orchestrated distinctive sensory experiences involving light and dark, imagery, space, sound and even altered states of consciousness (Bradley 1989a, 1989b; Thomas 1990, 1992; Lewis-Williams and Dowson 1993; Dronfield 1996; Watson and Keating 1999; Watson 2001b). In order to gain access it was necessary for participants to cross a threshold of large decorated stones that separated the wider world from the interior. Beyond these kerb-stones a confined passage led towards the chamber, a liminal place where encounters with death and the supernatural could be managed. Encounters with the monuments and landscape of Cumbria might also have entailed potent and possibly supernatural meanings. The high ground of the Lake District was itself a liminal and transcendent world where the rules of engagement between people and the environment were modified. In place of passage grave chambers were stone axe sources in the heart of the mountains, these 'altered' landscapes existing somewhere between natural places and formal monuments. The restricted access and extraordinary circumstances under which the axes were procured and shaped carries an element of theatre, a term that can be equally appropriate to describe monumental buildings. In this context, the discovery of a highly unusual panel of rock art in Great Langdale assumes an added dimension (Brown and Brown 1999; Beckensall 2002). Like Long Meg and Her Daughters, these motifs are best viewed by an audience oriented towards the mountainous interior of the Lake District, and it is probably no coincidence that the major stone axe quarries upon the Langdale Pikes constitute the focus of the vista. The motifs were incised onto a vertical surface, treating an outcrop as if it were a monument. They also create a frieze around large boulders that are suggestive of a stone façade and enclosed passageway which is aligned along the axis of the valley. Like rock art in the Vale of Eden, their composition and style has much in common with passage grave decoration.

Describing landscapes using ideas and terminology that might ordinarily be attributed to monuments need not be a dichotomy. Indeed, natural features in some regions might sometimes have been understood as built architecture (Bradley 1998b). Encounters with both passage graves or the Cumbrian landscape can be described in terms of ritualised or ceremonial actions, entailing separation from the everyday world, a time of liminality, followed by a process of re-incorporation back into society (van Gennep 1960; Turner 1969). The stone circles and henges to the north-east of the Lake District might have acted as an interface between two quite different worlds. Like the deepest spaces within passage graves, the axe sources were liminal and difficult to reach, and in both cases, specialised knowledge might have been a prerequisite for access.

While the population of Cumbria did not build passage graves, sites in the Vale of Eden might have been empowered with the memories of these influential buildings in Ireland. Such references might have been implicit in the winter solstice alignment at Long Meg and Her Daughters, where the setting sun not only moves into alignment with the decorated outlying monolith, but also the direction of Ireland (Bradley 1998c). There are other possibilities: the locations of Castlerigg, Long Meg and Her Daughters, Mayburgh and King Arthur's Round Table could arguably reproduce the hilltop/riverine contrasts between passage graves and enclosures in the Boyne Valley, and the Vale of Eden itself shares qualities with that landscape.

The interpretations we have suggested need not imply that all the Cumbrian sites were contemporary with Irish passage graves. The chronology of the stone circles and Mayburgh remains uncertain, but comparisons with sites elsewhere are suggestive of the third millennium BC (Burl 2000). In this respect, ideas concerning the Irish monuments might have taken the form of memories rather than contemporary accounts. Indeed, the decorated kerb-stones that marked the perimeters of the passage graves were the very parts of these monuments that could have been seen and referenced long after the interiors had been sealed.

CONCLUSIONS

Cumbria was one of a number of regions where ideas from other places and times converged. The Vale of Eden has more in common with places in Ireland such as the Boyne Valley than it does with neighbouring areas of northern England. Furthermore, these references seem to have been translated and assimilated into a region that had no history of passage grave construction. Yet the distinctive ways in which these influential Irish monuments structured space might have become enshrined within a cosmological scheme which operated at many different scales. Qualities of *both* mounds and enclosures were integrated at Mayburgh, and open circles were decorated in the manner of Irish passage graves. In the Irish tradition, such motifs frequently emphasised thresholds and boundaries, and perhaps places like these emphasised the contrasting topography between the lowlands and the mountains of the Lake District. Rather like entering the inner space of a passage grave, the ways in which people engaged with the Lake District mountains was quite different to the lowlands, and it was from these liminal places between the earth and the sky that stone axes were obtained. Indeed, the interior of the Lake District does not seem to have been permanently settled until the Bronze Age.

Cumbria may now be on the edge of England, but by tracing the ideas that circulated across the British Isles during the Neolithic we can see that this might not always have been the case. If we recall the analogy of Dalriada, the sea might have been a connection to symbols that had their ultimate origins in the east of Ireland.

ACKNOWLEDGEMENTS

We would like to thank Stan Beckensall and Paul Brown for information regarding rock art in Great Langdale, and Elizabeth Shee Twohig for her comments. Fieldwork was conducted at the Cumbrian monuments by Aaron Watson as part of a Ph.D. funded by the University of Reading and the British Academy.

Bibliography

Beckensall, S., 1999, *British prehistoric rock art*. Stroud. Tempus.
Beckensall, S., 2002, *Prehistoric Rock Art in Cumbria*. Stroud. Tempus.
Bloch, M., 1995, People into places: Zafimaniry concepts of clarity. In E. Hirsch and M. O'Hanlon (eds), *The anthropology of landscape*. Oxford. Clarendon Press. 63–77.
Bradley, R., 1989a, Darkness and light in the design of megalithic tombs. *Oxford Journal of Archaeology*, 8, 251–259.
Bradley, R., 1989b, Deaths and entrances: a contextual analysis of megalithic art. *Current Anthropology*, 30, 68–75.
Bradley, R., 1997, *Rock art and the prehistory of Atlantic Europe*. London. Routledge.
Bradley, R., 1998a, *The significance of monuments*. London. Routledge.
Bradley, R., 1998b, Ruined buildings, ruined stones: enclosures, tombs and natural places in the Neolithic of south-west England. *World Archaeology*, 30, 13–22.
Bradley, R., 1998c, Directions to the dead. In L. Larsson and B. Stjernqvist (eds), *The World View of Early Man*. Lund. Almqvist and Wiksell. 123–135.
Bradley, R., 1999, The stony limits - rock carvings in passage graves and in the open air. In A. Harding (ed.), *Experiment and design: archaeological studies in honour of John Coles*. Oxford. Oxbow. 30–36.
Bradley, R., 2000a, *The good stones: a new investigation of the Clava Cairns* (Society of Antiquaries of Scotland Monograph Series 17). Edinburgh. Society of Antiquaries of Scotland
Bradley, R., 2000b, *An archaeology of natural places*. London. Routledge.
Bradley, R. and Edmonds, M., 1993, *Interpreting the axe trade: production and exchange in Neolithic Britain*. Cambridge. Cambridge University Press.
Brown, P. and Brown, B., 1999, Previously unrecorded prehistoric rock carving at Copt Howe, Chapel Stile, Great Langdale, Cumbria. *Archaeology North*, 16, 16-18.
Burl, A., 1976, *The stone circles of the British Isles*. London. Yale University Press.
Burl, A., 1988, Coves: structural enigmas of the Neolithic. *Wiltshire Archaeological and Natural History Magazine*, 82, 1–18.
Burl, A., 2000, *The stone circles of Britain, Ireland and Brittany*. London. Yale University Press.
Campbell, E., 2001, Were the Scots Irish? *Antiquity*, 75, 285–292.
Claris, P. and Quartermaine, J., 1989, The Neolithic quarries and axe factory sites of Great Langdale and Scafell Pike: a new field survey. *Proceedings of the Prehistoric Society*, 55, 1–25.
Collins, A. E. P., 1957, Excavations at the Giant's Ring, Ballynahatty. *Ulster Journal of Archaeology*, 20, 44–50.

Collins, P. and Waterman, D., 1955, *Millin Bay: a late Neolithic cairn in Co. Down*. Belfast. HMSO.

Dronfield, J., 1996, Entering alternative realities: cognition, art and architecture in Irish passage-tombs. *Cambridge Archaeological Journal*, 6, 37–72.

Eogan, G., 1986, *Knowth and the Passage-Tombs of Ireland*. London. Thames and Hudson.

Ferguson, C., 1895, On a tumulus at Old Parks, Kirkoswald. *Transactions of the Cumberland and Westmorland Antiquarian and Archaeological Society*, 13, 389-399.

Frodsham, P., 1989, Two newly discovered cup and ring marked rocks from Penrith and Hallbankgate, with a gazetteer of all known megalithic carvings in Cumbria. *Transactions of the Cumberland and Westmorland Antiquarian and Archaeological Society*, 89, 1–19.

Hartwell, B., 1998, The Ballnahatty complex. In A. Gibson and D. Simpson (eds), *Prehistoric ritual and religion*. Stroud. Sutton. 32–44.

Lewis-Williams, J. D. and Dowson, T. A., 1993, On vision and power in the Neolithic: evidence from the decorated monuments. *Current Anthropology*, 34, 55–65.

Masters, L., 1984, The Neolithic long cairns of Cumbria and Northumberland. In R. Miket and C. Burgess (eds), *Between and beyond the walls*. Edinburgh. John Donald. 52–73.

O'Kelly, M. J., 1982, *Newgrange: archaeology, art and legend*. London. Thames and Hudson.

Richards, C., 1996, Monuments as landscape: creating the centre of the world in late Neolithic Orkney. *World Archaeology*, 28, 190–208.

Soffe, G. and Clare, T., 1988, New evidence of ritual monuments at Long Meg and Her Daughters, Cumbria. *Antiquity*, 62, 552–557.

Taçon, P., 1991, The power of stone: symbolic aspects of stone use and tool development in western Arnhem Land, Australia. *Antiquity*, 65, 192–207.

Thomas, J., 1990, Monuments from the inside: the case of the Irish megalithic tombs. *World Archaeology*, 22, 168–178.

Thomas, J., 1992, Monuments, movement, and the context of megalithic art. In N. Sharples and A. Sheridan (eds), *Vessels for the ancestors: essays on the Neolithic of Britain and Ireland*. Edinburgh. Edinburgh University Press. 143–155.

Topping, P., 1992, The Penrith henges: a survey by the Royal Commission on the Historical Monuments of England. *Proceedings of the Prehistoric Society*, 58, 249–264.

Tuan, Y., 1977, *Space and place: the perspective of experience*. London. Edward Arnold.

Turner, V., 1969, *The ritual process*. Chicago. Aldine.

van Gennep, A., 1960, *The rites of passage*. London. Routledge.

Waterhouse, J., 1985, *The stone circles of Cumbria*. Chichester. Phillimore.

Watson, A., 1995, Investigating the distribution of Group VI debitage in the central Lake District. *Proceedings of the Prehistoric Society*, 61, 461–462.

Watson, A. 2000, *Encircled space: the experience of stone circles and henges in the British Neolithic*. Unpublished Ph.D. thesis. University of Reading.

Watson, A., 2001a, Composing Avebury. *World Archaeology*, 33, 296–314.

Watson, A., 2001b, The sounds of transformation: acoustics, monuments and ritual in the British Neolithic. In N. Price (ed.), *The archaeology of shamanism*. London. Routledge. 178–192.

Watson, A. and Keating, D., 1999, Architecture and sound: an acoustic analysis of megalithic monuments in prehistoric Britain. *Antiquity*, 73, 325–336.

Chapter 7

No-man's land revisited:
some patterns in the Neolithic of Cumbria

Tom Clare

INTRODUCTION

The location of Cumbria at the geographical centre of the British Isles suggests that it should be an ideal place to study ideas of 'core', 'peripherality' and regionality (Figure 7.1). For example, while the 'trade' in group VI stone axes might be seen as reflecting the county's core position, its peripheral location, allowing for the assimilation of ideas from various regions, may have led to local distinctiveness and novel artefacts and monuments. However,

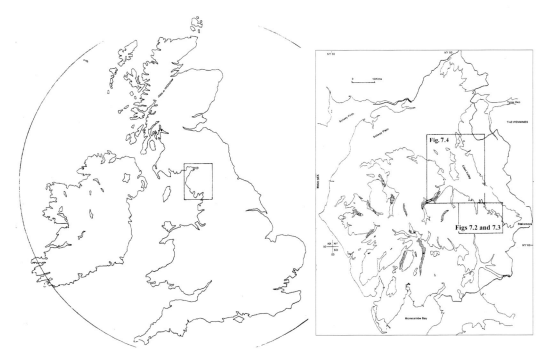

Figure 7.1 How the geographical position of Cumbria made it potentially both a core and peripheral are. (The centre of the large circle is the Langdale Pikes).

the identification of boundaries between 'regions' requires knowledge of other areas so that the process of identifying regionality or distinctiveness is a comparative one. For that reason any discussion of the available data must include evidence from adjacent areas and in that context a subtitle of this paper might be 'on the edge of Scotland'. Certainly it is necessary to recognise that the lowlands around Carlisle are topographically a continuation of those of lower Nithsdale and Annandale in south-west Scotland, an area that will be referred to as the Dumfries-Lockerbie lowland.

The purpose of this paper is, therefore, to identify any novel or preferred monuments and practices and to explore the linkages between Cumbria and other areas. In doing so, however, it is necessary to note that a basic problem in the Cumbrian Neolithic – and one which has undoubtedly contributed to the idea of a Neolithic 'no-man's land' (Frodsham 1996) – is the relative dearth of excavated sites and even fewer radiocarbon dates. In practice this means that assigning sites and information to the Neolithic period is often based on analogy or comparison with data sets in other regions and the inevitable consequence is that it is extremely difficult to identify novel, regional forms. It is therefore necessary to begin by re-examining the available data; some of which has long been accepted as being Neolithic in date and some of which has previously been consigned to other periods.

RECOGNISING THE ORTHODOX AND NOVEL IN SOME OF THE AVAILABLE DATASETS

Burial mounds and related sites

The issues raised are demonstrated by a consideration of 'long barrows' of which two, possibly three, have been excavated: Rayseat Pike (Greenwell 1877, 510–3); Skelmore Head (Powell 1963) and White Lyne (Richardson and Fell 1975, 20–2). Although no datable evidence exists for these sites the excavation accounts suggest they contained chamber-like areas which, in the case of Rayseat Pike, recall those found in sites in Eastern Yorkshire (Manby 1970), at Street House in Cleveland (Vyner 1984) and at Lochhill on the edge of the Dumfries-Lockerbie lowland (Masters 1973). It is, therefore, perhaps significant that Rayseat Pike is located in that part of Cumbria where topography allows – perhaps dictates – communication with all three areas, but with Yorkshire and Cleveland in particular.

At Rayseat Pike, Skelmore Heads and Lochhill, however, it is possible to interpret the details as marking the development of megalithic structures from timber ones. In that connection paired standing stones with vestigial or associated mounds, as at Kirksanton and Clifton (Fairclough (1979) for the latter), might represent a further development. At Kirksanton on the south-west coastal strip there were other stones 'placed in a rude manner' (Hutchinson 1794, vol. I, 530) and an air photograph hints at a surrounding circle of pits, so that the overall form of the monument might have been similar to that of the Street House 'Wossit' (Vyner 1988), while at Clifton in the Eden valley the stones were sometimes referred to as a cromlech.

Unlike south-west Scotland and the Isle of Man, no certain megalithic tombs are known in Cumbria. In the vicinity of Morecambe Bay, upright limestone slabs at Burton in Kendal and a 'lost' site in Furness can, however, be interpreted as the remains of simple chambers by those desperate to identify such sites. Similarly, the present form of the long cairn of Samson's Bratful on the western side of the Lake District and two long cairns on the Bewcastle Fells have been claimed to be the result of megalithic chambers being removed by persons unknown at times unknown. On the other hand the geographical proximity of the last two sites to south-west Scotland is worth noting as is the fact that Samson's Bratful lies on the western side of the Lake District massif, facing the Isle of Man.

A further link between south-west Scotland and Rayseat Pike is, however, suggested by the fact that the site can be described morphologically as two round cairns (Clare 1979) and in that respect the site recalls Mid Gleniron I in Wigtownshire where the long mound (with megalithic chambers) had developed from two round cairns (Corcoran 1969). It is, therefore, necessary to recognise that within Cumbria as elsewhere a tradition of building round cairns may have predated or existed alongside the building of rectilinear mounds (see Harding 1996 for this situation in eastern Yorkshire).

The existence in Cumbria of Neolithic round barrows comparable to those of Yorkshire has been demonstrated by Kinnes (1979) and to his list can be added sites like Old Parks and 45g on Moor Divock (RCHM 1936, 27) which had 'facades' echoing the eastern arrangements at Rayseat Pike (Clare 1979), Sizergh Fell and Asby Mask. On Sizergh Fell the excavator found an internal bank and pavement on and above which were burials (McKenny Hughes 1904) and at Asby Mask there were just three skulls 'in good preservation and entire' (Hodgson 1814, 152; RCHM 1936, 20). In addition to these, there are three sites where cists appear to have been designed for repeated access from above in a way recalling the first chamber at Cairnholy I (Scott 1969). The point to be made here is that such sites represent a local development, while Old Parks and Moor Divock suggest that local development was contemporary with Yorkshire.

However, the identification of these and other round barrows as Neolithic is complicated by the apparent survival of excarnation into the Bronze Age. Evidence for this practice has been demonstrated by modern excavation of ring cairns at Oddendale (Turnbull and Walsh 1997) and at nearby Hardendale (Williams and Howard-Davies 2004). That the tradition may also have included the subsequent cremation of the bones is suggested by burning on the platforms at Hardendale and by the evidence from the late Neolithic site of Beckton in the Dumfries-Lockerbie lowland (Pollard 1997, 116). Certainly such an interpretation is compatible with the possibility that the cremated bone found under the cairn adjacent to the Clifton standing stones were those of 'several individuals' (Fairclough 1979, 2). Moreover such a tradition may be related to the existence within Cumbria of multiple cremation cemeteries, either enclosed or unenclosed as at Aglionby near Carlisle. However similar sites are also recorded in south-west Scotland, the rest of north-west England and northern and eastern England. The majority of these sites are Bronze Age in date but they may have earlier origins, as a rim of Peterborough Ware and one of Impressed Ware of the kind found at Meldon Bridge exist in the material from Aglionby (Clare 1973, Figure 14d for the latter and Burgess 1976, 173 for a discussion of the principal characteristics of the type at Meldon Bridge and elsewhere).

Stone circles

Stone circles appear to represent one type of Cumbrian site which is relatively well known but it is necessary to note that the dating of sites is largely based on analogy and in particular on a free-standing typology. Attention is also drawn to the fact that there are within Cumbria what appears to be a number of different 'types' of stone circle: for example 'large' diameter sites with tall standing stones, such as Long Meg, Castlerigg, Gamelands and Swinside considered typologically to be early in date (Burl 1976); circles with similar diameters but with lower stones and central mounds, such as those at Seascale, Burnmoor, Gunnerkeld and Oddendale; and small diameter circles with central pits such as that at Broomrigg. However, classifying the sites is difficult because individual components may not belong to a single type. There is, for example, evidence of there having been mounds inside the circles at Castlerigg and Long Meg, while Gunnerkeld, Castlerigg, Swinside and Long Meg appear to have portal arrangements.

Nevertheless, there does appear to have been some regional diversity. In south-west Scotland, for example, Burl recognised three groups with, significantly, that centred on the Dumfries-Lockerbie lowland having 'large open circles' which 'may be of Cumbrian origin' (1976, 204). In contrast circles with central stones show a remarkable concentration to the west of the Dumfries-Lockerbie lowland (*ibid.*, Figure 37), although two possible examples might have existed in Cumbria. The first of these (Lacra D) was discussed by Burl but to that example might be added the largest circle on Burnmoor where a leaning stone (stone I in Figure 3 of Clare 1975) might have belonged to an earlier phase. Both sites are on the western side of the Lake District massif and the fact that some circles north of the Solway may have possessed central mounds also suggests that the regional diversity of monuments may not be as clear cut as appears at first.

A third aspect of stone circles which is relevant here is that, architecturally, Castlerigg, Long Meg and Swinside have features suggestive of palisaded enclosures such as those at Meldon Bridge and Dunragit in southern and south-western Scotland (Burgess 1976 and Thomas 2001, respectively). In this connection two concentric circles of timber posts dated to the late Neolithic have been identified at Oddendale (Turnbull and Walsh 1997) although it is noteworthy that the site was overlain not by a stone circle but by a ring cairn. It is also possible that the cropmark enclosure contiguous to Long Meg (Soffe and Clare 1988) may not be that of a ditched structure equivalent to that at Billown on the Isle of Man as has been suggested (Darvill 2001), but a wide palisade trench of the kind that existed at West Kennet (Whittle 1997, Figure 33). Similarly, the cropmarks recorded on the south-west coastal strip and interpreted as henges (Hodges *pers. comm.*) might be those of palisades.

Enclosures

Without evidence to the contrary, however, it is equally possible to interpret the Long Meg enclosure as being analogous to sites in Northern Ireland like Lyles Hill or nearby Donegore Hill (Sheridan 2001 for both), or Billown on the Isle of Man (Darvill 2001). Certainly it is necessary to recognise that enclosures comparable to those identified in other regions exist within the county. The majority of these have been listed by Oswald *et al.* (2001) but to those should be added the now destroyed site at Stone Close, Stainton, near to Skelmore

Heads. There, the finding of numerous stone (and bronze) axes led to the suggestion that the walls had formed a settlement 'like the Lyles Hill enclosure in Northern Ireland' (Manby 1965, 4) although a better analogy now might be Billown.

At Skelmore Heads itself the position of the 'long barrow' outside the putative enclosure is an arrangement seen at Hambledon Hill (Mercer 1988). Moreover, the Skelmore Heads enclosure, whether viewed as an earthwork or palisade, would have been defined by a cross-ridge boundary of the kind also existing at Hambledon Hill. In that context too, attention might be drawn to the existence of a 'cross ridge dyke' adjacent to the cremation cemetery at Ewanrigg, Maryport (Bewley *et al.* 1992 for the cemetery; Clare 2002 for the cross-ridge dyke) and to the fact that Vyner thought that they might be late Neolithic in date in north-east England (Vyner 1994; see also Darvill and Thomas 2001a, 13). In short, the situation in Cumbria is that described for Britain as a whole by Darvill and Thomas (*ibid.* 1–23): a number of possible Neolithic enclosures can be recognised and amongst these is a variety of forms.

Of the putative causewayed enclosures, that on Carrock Fell is the most interesting for it lies adjacent to the possible source of Group XXXIV axes (Fell and Davis 1988, 74) in a manner reminiscent of enclosures further south (*e.g.* Russell 1997 for Sussex). In addition the interrupted circuit is a bank and not a ditch; a situation which has implications for our understanding of which elements of classic causewayed enclosures were the most important.

It will be evident that the problems identified in the introduction are again apparent in this group of sites and the only securely dated site remains that of Plasketlands (Bewley 1993). Even there, however, the situation is not wholly clear for the radiocarbon dates relate to the rectilinear arrangement of posts and not the ditched enclosure that appeared contiguous but in uncertain stratigraphic relationship. It is, therefore, possible to suggest that the dated structure was similar to the 'pit-defined enclosures' of Scotland (Barclay 1997), significantly on the other side of the Solway from Plasketlands (*ibid.* Figure 8.2).

Stone axes

The procurement and distribution of stone axes and in particular those of Group VI have been the subject of a number of studies. Nevertheless, it is worth noting here that there is in general a correlation between concentrations of axes, whether finished or not, and all chance finds, and monuments. For example, the Long Meg complex is near, perhaps peripheral to, a concentration of axes, as is the enclosure at Plasketlands and, on the far side of the Solway, the monument(s) at Dunragit (Thomas 2001, 138–140).

At first sight, therefore, these patterns support the idea that stone circles and related monuments were in some way connected with the circulation of axes but there are no known comparable sites in the south-east of Cumbria – that area through which one might have expected material to have travelled to Yorkshire. Although the sites adjacent to Levens Park and Sizergh Fell south of Kendal are suggestive of an area in which one might begin to look for such sites (or their equivalent) the observed distributions might be better interpreted as the monuments being located in, or adjacent to, areas of Neolithic land use as represented by the axes. Such an interpretation is consistent with the very high concentration of axes in the Furness peninsula, where there are no known henges or early stone circles although few axes have been recovered from the coastal strip around Barfield Tarn, an area of demonstrable land use activity (below). On the other hand the latter is also an area of recorded stone circles and henge-like monuments and some other factors have affected the distribution of artefacts in that area (Clare *et al.* 2001).

It has been suggested above that the general distribution of axes relates to that of settlement (a view long ago suggested by Manby (1965)) and the hafted axe and other material recovered from Ehenside Tarn has always been interpreted in that way. No actual evidence of a settlement has, however, been found at Ehenside Tarn and a reinterpretation of the artefacts as representing votive offerings is possible. Such an interpretation would be consistent with the idea of votive offerings in general (Clare *et al.* in press for a similar interpretation of the axes from Portinscale, Keswick) and the recognition of artificial pools in Ireland (Hartwell 1994). In connection with the latter, the proximity of stone circles such as Castlerigg, Long Meg and Brats Hill on Burnmoor to bogs and former tarns might be noted; as indeed might the proximity of sites like Mayburgh to floodplains.

THE EVIDENCE OF THREE SPECIFIC AREAS

The limestone uplands of the upper Eden valley

Rayseat Pike, a number of Neolithic round barrows, the Gamelands stone circle and Shap avenue, the Oddendale circles and a putative 'causewayed enclosure' are located along with many Bronze Age sites on or adjacent to this escarpment. The area, which is largely unenclosed common land, has been the subject of fieldwalking and has produced a remarkable collection of lithics and pottery (Cherry and Cherry 1987). Within the material it is possible to recognise discrete patterns and those of relevance here can be summarised as:

- although local chert was used and beach flint would have been available on the western side of the Lake District, the flint used appears to have come from eastern Yorkshire (Cherry and Cherry 1996)
- there appears to have been continuity between late Mesolithic and early Neolithic sites
- the sites appear to avoid Bank Moor which palynology suggests had been kept free of trees by burning (Skinner and Brown 1999)
- the resource areas available for exploitation would, therefore, appear to have been the grassland of Bank Moor; areas of outcropping limestone pavement (which may or may not have carried woodland cover); areas of tarn, wetland and floodplain which may have carried reeds attractive to ungulates (Bay-Petersen 1978 for the latter in general); and areas of glacial soils with woodland cover
- it is in the latter area that the settlement sites are located (Figure 7.2a), presumably to maximise the extent of available grassland and reeds
- fragments of axes and flakes from polished stone tools are concentrated in the settlement areas while flakes of tuff and some flakes from polished stone implements occur beyond the settlement areas (Figure 7.2b)
- sites like Rayseat Pike do not appear to have any particular spatial relationship to the 'settlement' areas although the putative causewayed enclosure on Orton Scar suggests they may have been in peripheral positions

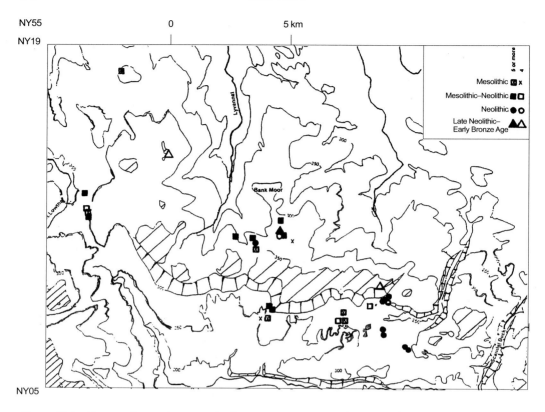

Figure 7.2a Core and periphery on the limestone escarpment between the rivers Eden and Lune: possible settlement sites indicated by 5 or more tool types.

- in the late Neolithic and early Bronze Age there is extensive expansion (or shift) into those areas not previously occupied but where flakes of tuff and polished stone tool were found (Figure 7.3).

It is not clear whether these settlements were seasonal or not but their size suggest they were and it is probable they were used in conjunction with the lowland where monuments like Mayburgh and Long Meg are located. This should not, however, be seen as necessarily indicative of mobility of the kind envisaged by Thomas (*e.g.* 1999, 222–3), for later sedentary farming within the Eden valley used and continues to use both enclosed 'bottom land' and unenclosed commons, such as those on the limestone escarpment. Nor does it preclude the seasonal movement of farming livestock being a development of a Mesolithic regime.

The central Eden valley

The pattern of expansion in the late Neolithic and Bronze Age noted above might also be recognised in the overall distribution of sites on the lower ground of the central Eden valley (Figure 7.4). However, that distribution also shows discrete groupings of monuments:

NY05

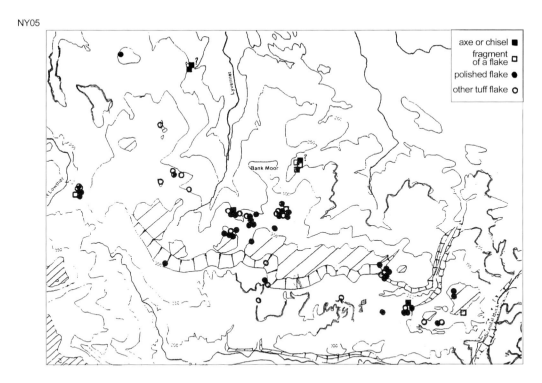

Figure 7.2b Core and periphery on the limestone escarpment between the rivers Eden and Lune: the distribution of fragments and flakes from possible axes.

Moor Divock, Mayburgh, Long Meg and Broomrigg (Table 7.1). A notable feature of these groupings is that they tend to possess different monument types, although the known distribution of cup-and-ring-decorated stones from this area occur in two groupings (Long Meg and Mayburgh). Nevertheless, the overall impression is that the groupings of sites were deliberately different, as if they were built by communities vying with each other and wishing to express and assert their own identities: an interpretation which does not preclude a hierarchy of community obligations and groupings. A similar situation has been noted in eastern Yorkshire (Harding 1996) and south-west Scotland (Burl 1976, 204) and the conclusion to be drawn is that distinctiveness occurs at a variety of scales – local as well as regional. In that context the sites recorded in Nithsdale (Barclay 1997, Figure 7.2) might be seen as simply another discrete grouping within the Eden-Dumfries-Lockerbie lowlands.

The south-west coastal strip

Here the pattern of settlement and land use appears to be similar to that on the limestone escarpment of the Eden valley:

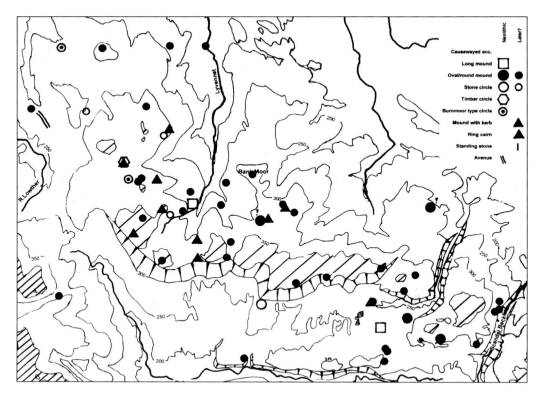

Figure 7.3 The distribution of Neolithic and Early Bronze Age monuments in the same area as Figure 7.2.

	Broomrigg	Long Meg	Mayburgh	Moor Divock
Stone circle > 30m diameter				
Stone circle > 30m diameter	1			
with outlier		1		
Henge				
Class I	1		1	
Class II			1	
Other			1	
Other enclosure		1		
Standing stone	1			1
Natural boulder	1			

Table 7.1 Known elements in principal site groupings in central Eden Valley.

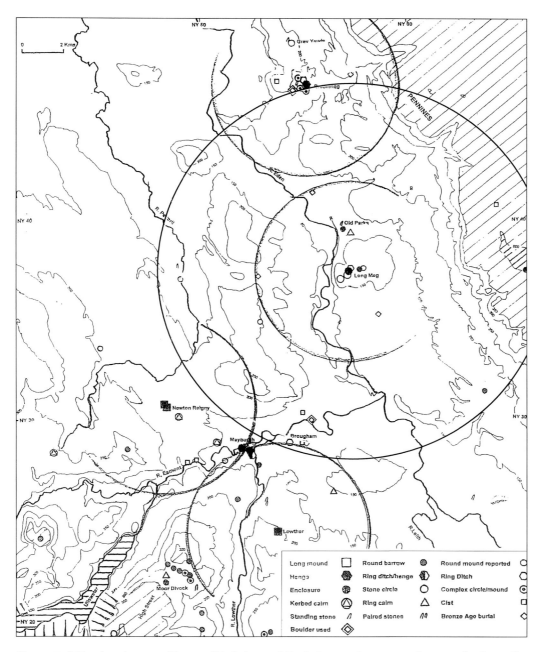

Figure 7.4 The distribution of known Neolithic and Early Bronze Age sites in the central Eden valley showing how groupings of sites might be regarded as being either core or peripheral or both.

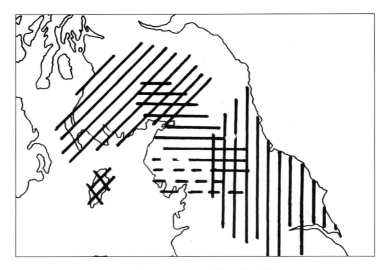

Figure 7.5 Linkages suggested by Neolithic mounds.

- continuity between late Mesolithic and early Neolithic is suggested in the vicinity of Eskmeals (Cherry and Cherry 1996)
- expansion of landuse in the late Neolithic is suggested by sediments (evidence described in Clare *et al.* 2001)
- that expansion appears to be reflected in the known distribution of monuments
- some evidence for the exploitation of both lowland and upland resources also exists, with stone circles and henge-like sites recorded on the lower ground and stone circles like the Lacra grouping on higher ground.

However, unlike on the limestone escarpment the source of flint used here was from the local beach (Cherry and Cherry 1996).

DISCUSSION AND CONCLUSIONS

The above review of *available* evidence demonstrates that, when monuments and objects of exchange are considered, Cumbria shared links with Yorkshire, south-west Scotland and beyond, and it could, therefore, be argued that the model suggested in Figure 7.1 is supported. However, similarities in monuments, for example between Rayseat Pike, Lochhill and Street House, can be interpreted as resulting from a common, shared ancestry. They are also compatible with a spatial and temporal trajectory of development in which the timber facades and mortuary structures of the eastern coast are adopted in the Eden valley and Dumfries-Lockerbie lowland as part of that shared ancestry and whilst there undergoing changes which led to or facilitated, in south-west Scotland, the building of megalithic tombs.

The model suggested by Figure 7.1 might therefore be better replaced with that in Figure 7.5 where it is envisaged that a greater diversity of forms and practices emerged during the

Neolithic. As such the new 'model' appears to be compatible with the evidence elsewhere, as on the nearby Isle of Man (Darvill 2001, 157). In Cumbria a small group of locally distinctive round cairns, such as those with open cists or the site at Old Parks, appear to be contemporary with other round barrows that had features similar to those found in Yorkshire (Kinnes 1979, for the latter). Similarly, the henge of King Arthur's Round Table, so similar to sites found elsewhere in Britain, occurs at a time when both locally discrete groupings occur in the Eden valley and when regional preferences in stone circles can be detected. Indeed, the existence of the unusual Mayburgh henge alongside the wholly 'classic' King Arthur's Round Table highlights an apparent duality of inspirations, motivations and sources: regional forms and diversity occurring alongside 'national' monument forms such as Class II henges.

The explanation for this duality may in part lie in the wish of local communities to express their own identity while possessing and fulfilling wider obligations. Certainly the form of monuments – including changes to them – must have been a matter of choice by existing communities and this conclusion is consistent with the evidence on the limestone escarpment and south-west coastal strip where the monuments appear to be separate from and superimposed on the landuse. In that sense the observed situation is similar to that of later prehistory where artefacts of trans-regional character most easily expressed in art styles such as 'la Tene' are possessed or adopted by, or superimposed upon, existing and evolving communities, and the explanation for the latter might well provide a model for our understanding of the Neolithic.

Whatever the explanation, it is apparent that spatial patterns that might be interpreted as 'core' or 'periphery' exist in and change with time. Figure 7.5 is based on one group of monuments ('burial' mounds) and different types of monuments may have different patterns. It is, therefore, necessary to ask whether diversity (whether spatial and/or temporal) is the same as regionalism and to note that even amongst present day communities with a strong sense of 'regional identity' the latter is difficult to map in the physical world. Attempts to map present landscape and ecological character and diversity are based on spatial groupings of attributes so that in Figure 7.5 the Dumfries-Lockerbie lowland is differentiated from adjacent areas of southern Scotland and the Eden valley. Such distributions will, however, reflect and change with time but scale is an issue and patterns of diversity might vary with scale. The archaeological record, therefore, consists of discrete groupings of attributes the distribution of which change or remain unchanged through time so that the 'region' is constantly redefined.

Bibliography

Barclay, G. J., 1997, The Neolithic. In K. J. Edwards and I. B. M. Ralston (eds), *Scotland: Environment and Archaeology, 8000BC–AD1000.* Chichester. Wiley and Sons. 127–150.

Bay-Petersen, J. L., 1978, Animal exploitation in Mesolithic Denmark. In P. Mellars (ed.), *The early postglacial settlement of Northern Europe.* London. Duckworth. 115–146.

Bewley, R. H., 1993, Survey and Excavation at a Crop-Mark Enclosure, Plasketlands, Cumbria. *Transactions of the Cumberland and Westmorland Antiquarian Society*, XCIII, 1–18.

Bewley, R. H., Longworth, I. H., Browne, S., Huntley, J. P. and Varndell, G., 1992, Excavation of a Bronze age cemetery at Ewanrigg, Maryport, Cumbria. *Proceedings of the Prehistoric Society*, 58, 325–354.

Burgess, C., 1976, Meldon Bridge: a Neolithic defended promontory complex near Peebles. In C. Burgess and R. Miket (eds), 151–180.

Burgess, C. and Miket, R., 1976, *Settlement and Economy in the 3rd and 2nd Millenium BC* (= BAR British Series 33). Oxford. British Archaeological Reports.

Burl, A., 1976, *The Stone Circles of the British Isles*. Yale. Yale University Press.

Cherry, J. and Cherry, P. J., 1987, *Prehistoric Habitation Sites on the Limestone Uplands of Eastern Cumbria* (= Transactions of the Cumberland and Westmorland Antiquarian and Archaeological Society Research Series Volume II).

Cherry, P. and Cherry, J., 1996, Coastline and Upland in the Cumbrian Neolithic. In P Frodsham (ed.), 61–67.

Clare, T., 1973, *Stone circles and kindred monuments of North West England*. Unpublished MA Thesis. University of Liverpool.

Clare, T., 1975, Some Cumbrian stone circles in perspective. *Transactions of the Cumberland and Westmorland Antiquarian Society*, LXXV, 1–16.

Clare, T., 1979, Rayset Pike Long Cairn in the Machell MSS. *Transactions of the Cumberland and Westmorland Antiquarian Society*, LXXIX, 144–146.

Clare, T., 2002, Two prehistoric boundary types previously unrecorded in Cumbria. *Transactions of the Cumberland and Westmorland Antiquarian Society*, 3rd Series, II, 21–28.

Clare, T., Clapham, A. J., Wilkinson, D. M. and Haworth, E. Y., 2001, The Mesolithic and Neolithic landscapes of Barfield Tarn and Eskmeals in the English Lake District: some new evidence from two different wetland contexts. *Journal of Wetland Archaeology*, 1, 83–105.

Clare, T., Clapham, A. J., Wilkinson, D. M. and Taylor, J. J., 2002, The context of the stone axes found at Portinscale in the vicinity of Castlerigg stone circle. Neolithic settlement site or a case of votive offerings? *Archaeological Journal*, 159, 242–248.

Corcoran, J. X. W. P., 1969, Excavation of two chambered cairns at Mid Gleniron Farm, Glenluce, Wigtownshire. *Transactions of the Dumfriesshire and Galloway Natural History and Antiquarian Society*, 46, 29–90.

Darvill, T., 2001, Neolithic enclosures in the Isle of Man. In T. Darvill and J. Thomas 2001b (eds), 155–170.

Darvill, T. and Thomas, J., 2001a, Neolithic enclosures in Atlantic northwest Europe: some recent trends. In T. Darvill and J. Thomas (eds), 1–23.

Darvill, T. and Thomas, J., 2001b, (eds), *Neolithic Enclosures in Atlantic Northwest Europe*. (Neolithic Studies Group seminar papers 6). Oxford. Oxbow.

Fairclough, G. J., 1979, Excavation of standing stones and cairn at Clifton, Cumbria, 1977. *Transactions of the Cumberland and Westmorland Antiquarian Society*, LXXIX, 1–4.

Fell, C. I. and Davis, R. V., 1988, The petrological identification of stone implements from Cumbria. In T. H. M. Clough and W. A. Cummins (eds), *Stone Axe Studies Volume 2* (CBA Research Report No 67). London. CBA. 71–77.

Frodsham, P., 1996, *Neolithic Studies in No-Man's Land* (Northern Archaeology 13/14). Newcastle: Northern Archaeology Group.

Greenwell, W., 1877, *British Barrows*. Oxford. Clarendon Press.

Harding, J., 1996, Reconsidering the Neolithic Round Barrows of Eastern Yorkshire. In P. Frodsham (ed.), 67–78.

Hartwell, B., 1994, Late Neolithic ceremonies. *Archaeology Ireland*, 30, 10–13.

Hodgson, J., 1814, *Beauties of England and Wales, Westmorland*. London.

Hutchinson, W., 1794, *The History of the County of Cumberland*. Carlisle. F Jollie.

Kinnes, I., 1979, *Round Barrows and Ring-ditches in the British Neolithic* (British Museum Occasional paper 7). London. British Museum.

Manby, T. G., 1965, The distribution of rough-out, "Cumbrian" and related stone axes of Lake

District origin in Northern England. *Transactions of the Cumberland and Westmorland Antiquarian and Archaeological Society*, LXV, 1–52.

Manby, T. G., 1970, Long barrows of northern England: structural and dating evidence. *Scottish Archaeological Forum*, 2, 1–27.

Masters, L., 1973, The Lochhill long cairn. *Antiquity*, 47, 96–100.

McKenny Hughes, T., 1904, On another *tumulus* on Sizergh Fell. *Transactions of the Cumberland and Westmorland Antiquarian and Archaeological Society*, IV, 201–204.

Mercer, R. J., 1988, Hambledon Hill, Dorset, England. In C. Burgess, P. Topping, C. Mordant, and M. Maddison (eds), *Enclosures and defences in the Neolithic of western Europe* (BAR International series 403). Oxford. British Archaeological Reports. 89–106.

Oswald, A., Dyer, C. and Barber, M., 2001, *The creation of monuments: Neolithic causewayed enclosures in the British Isles*. Swindon. English Heritage.

Pollard, T., 1997, Excavation of a Neolithic settlement and ritual complex at Beckton Farm, Lockerbie, Dumfries and Galloway. *Proceedings of the Society of Antiquaries of Scotland*, 127, 69–121.

Powell, T. G. E., 1963, Excavations at Skelmore Heads near Ulverston, 1957 and 1959. *Transactions of the Cumberland and Westmorland Antiquarian and Archaeological Society*, LXIII, 1–30.

RCHM, 1936, *An inventory of the historical monuments in Westmorland*. London. HMSO.

Richardson, G. G. S. and Fell, C. I., 1975, Unpublished excavations by the late Miss K. S. Hodgson, F.S.A.. *Transactions of the Cumberland and Westmorland Antiquarian and Archaeological Society*, LXXV, 17–28.

Russell, M., 1997, NEO-"Realism?": An alternative look at the chalkland database of Sussex. In P. Topping (ed.), *Neolithic Landscapes* (= Neolithic Studies Group Seminar Papers 2). Oxford. Oxbow. 60–76.

Scott, J., 1969, The Clyde Cairns of Scotland. In T. G. E. Powell, J. W. X. P. Corcoran, F. Lynch and J. Scott (eds), *Megalithic Enquiries in the West of Britain*. Liverpool. Liverpool. University Press. 175–122.

Sheridan, A., 2001, Donegore Hill and other Irish Neolithic enclosures: a view from outside. In T. Darvill and J. Thomas 2001b (eds), 171–189.

Skinner, C. and Brown A. G., 1999, Mid-Holocene vegetation diversity in eastern Cumbria. *Journal of Biogeography*, 26, 45–54.

Soffe, G. and Clare, T., 1988, New evidence of ritual monuments at Long Meg and her Daughters, Cumbria. *Antiquity*, 62, 552–557.

Thomas, J., 1999, *Understanding the Neolithic*. London. Routledge.

Thomas, J., 2001, Neolithic enclosures: reflections on excavations on Wales and Scotland. In T. Darvill and J. Thomas 2001b (eds), 132–143.

Turnbull, P. and Walsh, D., 1997, A Prehistoric ritual sequence at Oddendale, near Shap. *Transactions of the Cumberland and Westmorland Antiquarian and Archaeological Society*, CVII, 11–44.

Vyner, B. E., 1984, The excavation of a Neolithic cairn at Street House, Loftus, Cleveland. *Proceedings of the Prehistoric Society*, 50, 151–196.

Vyner, B. E., 1988, The Street House Wossit: the excavation of a Late Neolithic and Early Bronze Age palisaded ritual monument at Street House, Loftus, Cleveland. *Proceedings of the Prehistoric Society*, 54, 173–202.

Vyner, B. E., 1994, The territory of ritual: cross-ridge boundaries and the prehistoric landscapes of the Cleveland Hills, northeast England. *Antiquity*, 68, 27–38.

Williams, J. and Howard-Davies, C., 2004, Excavations on a Bronze Age Cairn at Hardendale Nab, Cumbria, *Archaeological Journal* 161, 11–53

Whittle, A., 1997, *Sacred Mound Holy Rings*. Oxford. Oxbow.

Chapter 8

Core or periphery? The case of the Neolithic of the East Midlands

Patrick Clay

BACKGROUND

The origin of this paper lies in research into the Neolithic of the East Midlands claylands of Northamptonshire and Leicestershire and a subsequent widening of the study area as part of the Regional Research Frameworks exercise (Clay 2006). The region is defined as covering Northamptonshire, Leicestershire, Rutland, Lincolnshire, Nottinghamshire and Derbyshire – some 15,688km² (Figure 8.1). Within a region of this size it might be expected to include areas that by our modern definitions could be described as 'core' or 'periphery' during the Neolithic.

However the East Midlands do not figure greatly in Neolithic studies; with some notable exceptions, for example research in the Peak District (Hawke-Smith 1979; Bradley and Hart 1983), the Lincolnshire Wolds (*e.g.* Philips 1989; Jones 1998) and the Trent valley (*e.g.* Garton *et al.* 1989), it has been seen by many as a peripheral area. Areas which have traditionally been considered to have seen limited exploitation during the Neolithic include the extensive tracts of clayland – boulder clays, Liassic clays and Mercia mudstones – found in the region, which have generally been interpreted as peripheral areas in view of the perceived problems of cultivating heavy soils (*e.g.* Hall 1985). However recent research has questioned these assumptions (Clay 1996, 2002) and has suggested that many of these areas, with long subsequent histories of successful arable and pastoral farming, may have been equally attractive to early farming communities – the very success of which has made the identification of pre-Iron Age evidence more difficult (Mills 1985, 41).

This paper, therefore, is based on the following assumptions, some of which may appear obvious statements but are important caveats before attempts at defining regional distinctiveness are made:

- core areas in the Neolithic are likely to include those with long subsequent histories of arable and mixed farming – conspicuously absent from many of the areas discussed elsewhere in this volume;

- many areas with prominent evidence for Neolithic activity, for example Wessex, Orkney and the Boyne valley, are a product of survival and visibility. They may have been core areas during the Neolithic but not necessarily any more special than other areas, which have left less visible evidence. Much of their perceived status has been a result of the weight of research focused upon them (Barclay 2001). (The way in which certain areas

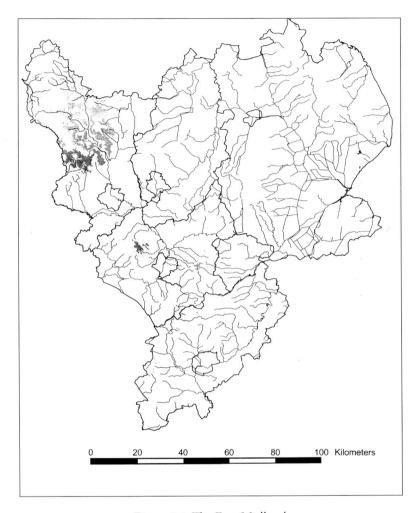

Figure 8.1 The East Midlands.

have dominated research conjures up the image of footballers chasing the ball instead of using all of the pitch);

- areas where monuments can be classified along traditional lines, for example henges, have received more attention than others where greater variation is present and classification less easy;

- some apparent regional distinctiveness may be illusory, especially when the perceived absence of monuments is used as an indicator. Despite progress in identifying areas of Neolithic activity we are far from seeing an unbiased picture; for example, aerial photography has been a powerful tool in locating monuments on some soils but is less successful on others. Field survey methodologies in use are not always of an appropriate resolution to detect Neolithic activity;

- some commentators have questioned whether arable farming and permanent settlement were significant aspects of Neolithic life (Thomas 1991, 28 and 1996; Barrett 1994) and the picture that has been presented is one in which Neolithic landscape and settlement is now characterised by mobility (Whittle 1997). However it can also be argued that mobility models are easier to interpret where visibility is limited (Cooney 1997; Rowley-Conwy 2000; Barclay 2001);

- core and periphery are modern concepts which were not necessarily relevant to Neolithic societies (Barclay 2001).

THE EAST MIDLANDS

In many ways the East Midlands does not form a coherent region (McCullagh 1969) and some areas fit better into other landscape zones: for example the Lincolnshire fens with their continuation into Cambridgeshire; the Derbyshire uplands with their counterparts in south Yorkshire; and north Staffordshire and the Trent valley with its upstream extension into south Staffordshire. However, examining a region of this size provides an opportunity to consider a wide range and variety of different landscape zones – in many ways a palimpsest of the landscape of Britain – crossing highland and lowland zones and including fen and coastal areas. A transect running north-west to south-east from the Derbyshire Peak uplands in the north-west of the region to the Lincolnshire fen-edge encompasses a wide range of different topographies and substrata including, for example, gritstone uplands, magnesium limestone, coal measures, Bunter sandstones, Trent river gravels and alluvium, Mercia mudstones, boulder clay, glacial gravels, Jurassic ridge limestones, Northampton Sand ironstones, Liassic clays, fen alluvium and Oxford clay. Neolithic communities in the region would, therefore, have exploited, to varying extents, a wide and distinctive range of contrasting environments.

With a few exceptions, such as the Derbyshire uplands, the region is dominated by areas of arable farmland. Furthermore, much of the region has seen successful agricultural exploitation since at least the Roman period which, together with urban development, opencast coal mining, gravel-, limestone-, and ironstone-quarrying, has had a considerable impact on the survival of the region's prehistory. This is highlighted by the data from Northamptonshire. About 75% of the county has been heavily ploughed; 12% quarried or damaged by urban development, while 6% is protected beneath alluvium or colluvium; thus only 2 to 3% has remained unploughed and undeveloped during medieval and modern times and would have potential for surviving pre-medieval earthworks (Kidd 1999).

Findspots, artefact scatters and cropmarks are the most common categories for the Neolithic in the Sites and Monuments Records (SMRs) for the six counties. With the exception of the Derbyshire Peak District, earthworks are rare but present within each of the counties in small numbers. These include long barrows on the Lincolnshire Wolds; a henge monument at Gunthorpe, Nottinghamshire; round barrows at Wakerly Wood and Woodford, Northamptonshire and at Lockington and Sproxton, Leicestershire. Important discoveries have also been made following geophysical survey (*e.g.* Husbands Bosworth

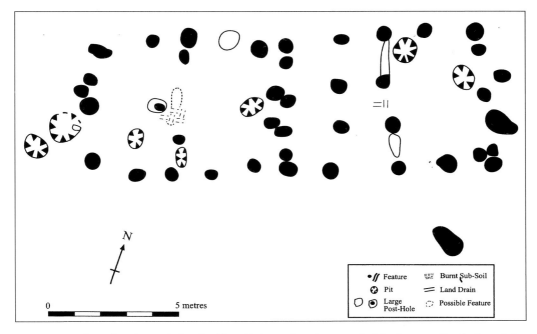

Figure 8.2 Plan of early Neolithic building(s) located at Lismore Fields, Buxton, Derbyshire (after Garton 1991).

causewayed enclosure, Leicestershire: Butler and Thomas 1999; Butler *et al.* 2002), trial trenching (Redlands Farm long barrow, Stanwick, Northamptonshire: Keevill 1992) and excavations (*e.g.* the ritual complex at West Cotton, Northamptonshire; Windell 1989) many of which have been discovered during work undertaken under PPG16.

In examining the evidence for the Neolithic (and other periods) it must be remembered that systematic survey has only been undertaken in a few areas and consideration of the SMR in isolation will reproduce inherent biases (Mills 1985). The subsoil of much of the area is not conducive to aerial reconnaissance (Pickering and Hartley 1985; Pickering 1989) and the potential of large areas of pasture and alluvium remains unknown. Therefore extrapolation and model-building from well-surveyed areas will, arguably, be a better basis for understanding how the area was exploited than using SMR-generated data alone. To assess the significance of the region during the Neolithic evidence of clearance, settlement, ceremonial and burial monuments and trading contacts are used as indicators.

NEOLITHIC SETTLEMENT

In contrast to many areas, there is evidence of Neolithic settlement from the region. The best-known site is at Lismore Fields, Buxton, Derbyshire (Figure 8.2; and see Garton 1991). Situated on boulder clay substratum within an upland basin formed by the Wye

Valley at 300m OD and surrounded on all sides by hills, the site consisted of a lithic and pottery assemblage associated with a group of features including sub-rectangular buildings with preserved floors, post holes and pits. Analysis of the ground plans has suggested that three similar structures are present. Charred plant remains from the buildings included emmer grains and chaff and flax seeds. A series of five radiocarbon dates ranging between 3990–3105 cal BC (95%) was obtained from this site.

Other more ephemeral settlement evidence is known from Aston, Derbyshire (Reaney 1968), Croft, Leicestershire (Hughes and Rosseff 1995), Dragonby, Lincolnshire (May 1976, 43), Ecton, Northamptonshire (Moore and Williams 1975), Great Ponton, Lincolnshire (Philips 1935) and Tattershall Thorpe, Lincolnshire (Chowne 1993). At Croft possible palisade gullies for post-ring roundhouses have been located in a low-lying stream and river-side areas close to the confluence of the Soar and Thurlaston Brook; on the basis of C14 and lithic evidence these can be dated to the early Neolithic (Hughes and Rosseff 1995, 105).

Late Neolithic settlement evidence has been examined at Swine Sty, Big Moor, Baslow, Derbyshire (Garton and Beswick forthcoming) and Aleck Low (Hart 1985; Garton 1991). Structures associated with field systems have also been located in north Derbyshire at Gibbet Moor, Gardoms Edge and Big Moor (Ainsworth 2001), while extensive field systems have been located on the eastern moors of the Peak District (Barnatt 1986, 1987). Other middle/late Neolithic settlement is known from Willington, south Derbyshire (Wheeler 1979, 58), Risby Warren, Lincolnshire (May 1976, 65–6), Ecton, Northamptonshire (Moore and Williams 1975), Elton, Northamptonshire (French 1991) and Stanton on the Wolds, Nottinghamshire (Bird and Bird 1972). Work in 2002 by Trent and Peak Archaeological Unit at Langford, Nottinghamshire has located pit and post hole features partly sealed beneath the Roman Fosse Way associated with bowl pottery, and Peterborough ware. Barley, spelt and hazelnut shells were present in pits sealed beneath the road agger (D. Knight pers. comm.).

Most Neolithic evidence, however, comes from surface scatters, 'site signatures' some of which may denote the presence of former settlement or associated activity. The region has developed a tradition of fieldwalking surveys with important pioneering work by, for example, Radley and Cooper (1968) in Derbyshire, Foard (1979) and Hall (1985) in Northamptonshire and Liddle (1985, 1994) in Leicestershire. Well-surveyed areas include the North Derbyshire transect survey (Myers 1991; Barnatt 1996), Kenslow, Derbyshire (Garton and Beswick 1983), the Fenland survey (Hayes and Lane 1992; Lane 1993), the Lincolnshire Wolds survey (Phillips 1989), the Bain valley survey (Chowne 1994), the Raunds Area Survey (Parry 1994, 2005) and the Medbourne Survey (Liddle 1994). This work has shown that lithic scatters containing early Neolithic material are widespread throughout the region including areas which have previously been regarded as remaining unoccupied until later periods such as the claylands in Northamptonshire, Leicestershire (Clay 1996, 2002) and Nottinghamshire (Bishop 1999) and the coal measures in Derbyshire (Garton 1995). A typical example is the Swift valley, a boulder clay area in south-west Leicestershire, where survey suggests Neolithic core area activity every 2 square km and produced lithic densities which are comparable with those from surveys of chalkland areas in the south of England including those in East Berkshire, the Maddle Farm area, Wiltshire and the Vale of White Horse (Ford 1987; Gaffney and Tingle 1989; Clay 1996, 1999, 2002).

Pollen and land snail faunal analyses of samples from ombrogenous peat bog, palaeochannel and buried soil deposits in the region provide some evidence of cleared landscapes during the early Neolithic (*e.g.* Hicks 1971, 1972; Clay 1981, 10 and 1999; Evans 1991; Wiltshire and Edwards 1993; Taylor *et al.* 1994; Brown 2000, 57). Of particular note is a pollen diagram from Collingham, Nottinghamshire that indicated the presence of cultivated cereals in a pre-Elm decline context (Bishop 1999) while cereal pollen is present in an immediately post-Elm decline diagram from Cottam, Nottinghamshire (Scaife and Allen 1999). In addition to the charred cereals from Lismore Fields (Garton 1991), emmer wheat seeds are recorded from Aston on Trent associated with Grimston ware pottery (Reaney 1968).

CEREMONIAL AND BURIAL MONUMENTS

A wide variety of Neolithic monuments is known from the region. Aerial photography has extended the distribution of causewayed enclosures into the Midland river valleys (Wilson 1975; Palmer 1976). Eight examples are known from the six counties comprising four from Lincolnshire at Uffington, Barholm, South Rauceby and Dowsby (May 1976), three from Northamptonshire at Briar Hill (Bamford 1985), Dallington (RCHME 1985, 30 and Figure 2) and Southwick (RCHME 1975, 86) and one from Husbands Bosworth, Leicestershire (Butler and Thomas 1999; Clay 1999, 7; Butler *et al.* 2002) while Gardoms Edge and Cranfield Rocks, Derbyshire (Ainsworth and Barnatt 1998; Barnatt and Smith 1997, 34; Makepeace 1999) may represent upland causewayed enclosures previously thought to be hillforts. Together with the Cambridgeshire causewayed enclosures at Etton, Northborough and Upton (Oswald *et al.* 2001, 149–150), the Welland group form part of a concentration of these monuments the density of which is matched only in Wessex and the Cotswolds (Butler *et al.* 2002, Figure 11.1). These may reflect evidence of a regional boundary or a place for cross regional contacts, although this apparent concentration may reflect the reliance on identifying these monuments from aerial photography, with more awaiting discovery.

A second group of early Neolithic monuments comprises long barrows, chambered cairns and long enclosures. These are relatively numerous in the region, especially in the Peak District. Of particular note are the fifth-millennium C14 dates (4360–3990 cal BC, 4310–3775 cal BC and 4075–3720 cal BC) from inhumations located within a chambered tomb, which was later incorporated into a long cairn at Whitwell, Derbyshire (Schulting 2000). Neolithic 'elongated' enclosures are known from other parts of the region including a chain of long enclosures spaced at intervals of 10.5 to 12.5 km along the Nene valley in Northamptonshire and west Cambridgeshire (Chapman 1997).

Cursus monuments are apparently largely absent from the region although examples are known as cropmark sites at Aston on Trent (Gibson and Loveday 1989; Garton and Elliot 1998), Willington (Potlock) in south Derbyshire (Wheeler 1970; Knight 1999) and Normanton on Soar in Nottinghamshire. Radiocarbon dates from excavations at Willington indicate an early third-millennium date for its construction (R. Loveday pers. comm). Jones (1998, 100) has suggested that the apparent absence of cursus monuments in areas of the Midlands may be due to linear post/pit-alignment monuments being adopted as an alternative to cursus building. Examples of these alignments are suggested from Lincolnshire

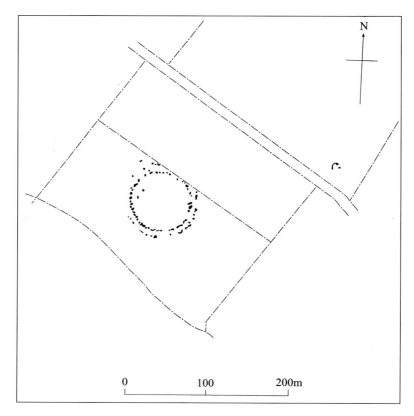

Figure 8.3 Cropmark of double post circle at East Stoke, Nottinghamshire.

at Steingot and Bag Enderby (*ibid.* 100). However, without excavation it is not easy to differentiate them from pit-alignments of later Bronze Age or Iron Age date.

While there are several examples of henge monuments from the region classifications such as 'henge' can be misleading and they should be seen as part of a broad tradition including a wide range of different form of ceremonial monument that can show considerable local variation (*e.g.* Clare 1986, 1987). There is the danger that henges showing the requisite banks and ditches receive more attention than other monuments with different construction methods that are likely to have been of similar status and function. An example of such a monument is the remarkably large post circle from East Stoke, Nottinghamshire (Harding and Lee 1987, 28–29), which would have formed an imposing structure 70m in diameter – comparable in scale to many large henges from other parts of Britain (Figure 8.3).

Numerous stone circles and ring cairns are known from the Derbyshire Peak (Barnatt 1990). Other post circles, besides the East Stoke example are known from Rearsby, Leicestershire (Clay 1999) and West Ashby, Lincolnshire (Field 1985). Pit circles include examples from Oakham, Rutland where there was a sequence of three enclosures demarcated by pits, associated with Peterborough ware, located next to a small ring-ditch surrounding a crouched burial (Clay 1998). It is likely that the pits originally marked the location of timber posts (Gibson 1994).

Although rarely considered as ceremonial monuments, some burnt mounds of Neolithic date have been identified from the region, which may be associated with river-edge ceremonial activities. An example of a middle Neolithic burnt mound with possible feasting evidence has been found at Willington in south Derbyshire (Beamish and Ripper 2000; Beamish 2001). This formed part of a complex of Trent floodplain activity comparable to similar evidence from Yarnton in the Thames valley (Hey 1997).

TRADING CONTACTS

There is evidence of the import of both raw materials and finished items into the region. For example, a distinctive range of elaborate artefacts has been noted from the Arbor Low area (Vine 1982; Bradley and Hart 1983) suggesting extensive contacts beyond the Peak. The Charnwood area is a source for the Group XX axes, although the exact location is unknown (Bradley 1989). Control of movement of these axes between the cursus/henge complexes at Aston and Willington in South Derbyshire and the Arbor Low area of the White Peak – a north-west passage along the Dove-Derwent corridor – has been suggested by Roy Loveday (2004.). The potential of the Peak as a copper resource would also repay attention: evidence of Bronze Age mining has been located nearby in the Ecton area of north Staffordshire (Barnatt and Thomas 1998).

DISCUSSION

The picture that is emerging is of a region being exploited extensively, and in some areas intensively, between the fifth and second millennium BC. Based on the information available from well-surveyed areas, contrasting models of upland and lowland Neolithic exploitation in the region can be suggested.

John Barnatt (1996) has re-interpreted some of the earlier research for the Peak District area and presented models of how Neolithic exploitation took place within (and between) four different topographical zones of the area. Early Neolithic groups passed through the landscape at different times of year along traditional paths. They were continuing a seasonal cycle which had occurred for many previous generations but which now included grazing domesticates in the same areas that were also favoured by wild species such as deer. Upland pasture areas would have been shared and the construction of chambered tombs would have identified places in the landscape, which had meaning to the groups who had created them. Where there is evidence which might suggest more 'permanent' settlement, for example the Lismore Fields site, this may not be incompatible with a more mobile community but may reflect the fact that many members of the community would not have needed to move with the flocks and herds (*ibid.*, 57 but see below).

A model can also be suggested for the less visible central lowlands including the clayland areas of Northamptonshire and Leicestershire (Clay 1996, 2002). The data here suggest that in many cases communities were using the same locations as later Mesolithic groups, close to the headwaters of streams and rivers. Following Barrett (1994), these groups may have gradually added non-intensive agricultural practices to their hunter-gatherer activities during the fourth millennium BC. During this time, from the distribution of lithic scatters, an expansion of occupation downstream from the 'core areas' located near to these headwaters appears to have taken place. Small-scale clearance allowed new areas to be cultivated, which, over time, led to a significant, if gradual, change in the landscape. The use of certain areas for more permanent settlement is perhaps suggested by the few communal monuments of this period, which were perhaps constructed at the interface of the groups' 'home ranges'. It is likely that the early Neolithic groups were still mobile with different areas used for different seasonal activities. Some occupation of low-lying confluences was taking place, perhaps for ritual activities (Brown 2000) with the interfluves only being exploited intermittently. By the late third–early second millennia BC, while seasonal movement to preferred pasturing areas was still taking place, there may have been longer maintenance of cleared land and more intensive 'short fallow' agriculture (Barrett 1994) with allocation of land for ritual and burial rites, sometimes respecting or re-using areas where communal monuments had been established in the early Neolithic. The late Neolithic 'core areas' are more commonly situated at a slightly lower altitude, further downstream than the early Neolithic sites.

CORE OR PERIPHERY?

So how does the East Midlands fit into core/periphery models or should such terms be used? Our modern definitions of core and periphery are not necessarily relevant to Neolithic societies. To a semi-mobile society the following would be considered equally important:

- where resources were procured (food-tools);
- access: the routes taken to procure these resources;
- where they met other groups;
- where (more recent) ancestors were buried;
- the uncleared forest – a memory that their more distant ancestors were forest dwellers – perhaps a place where their spirits still remained.

Their concept of space and access to a landscape will have been based on the historical knowledge of an area being passed down through different generations. This knowledge of previous events that had occurred within an area would influence how communities would exploit it. 'Good' experiences in an area might lead to an area being frequently re-used whereas 'bad' experiences might lead to the area being avoided. Historical knowledge might be reflected in the archaeological record where multi-period use of one location is detected. The historical knowledge of an area might also have a symbolic significance. Areas with their own 'mythology' or ritual importance might influence their interaction with different prehistoric groups (Mithen 1990).

To summarise, the evidence from this region varies in its quality and accessibility while visibility and sample bias mean that our picture of regional variation is incomplete. While the current models of Neolithic society emphasise mobility (Barrett 1994; Thomas 1996; Whittle 1997) there is the danger that this has become the new orthodoxy. This does appear to fit the evidence we have for much of the East Midlands but this may be more a reflection of visibility and survival rather than a true indication of the how the region was being exploited. For example when the Lismore Fields settlement was first discovered it was seen as a crucial breakthrough in early Neolithic studies. However, in view of the small number of sites with this type of information that has been located, it has been suggested (not entirely convincingly) that this site and the similar example from Balbridie (Fairweather and Ralston 1993) may have been non-typical or non-domestic (Thomas 1996). This is a perhaps a reflection of attempting to fit evidence into the mobility models which are currently in vogue and may say more about the rigidity of our models rather than accepting that the Lismore Fields evidence does appear to indicate early Neolithic settlement and arable cultivation (Garton 1991; Jones 2000). It can also be argued that the apparent absence of similar sites in many parts of Britain is due more to taphonomic factors and problems of visibility rather than a genuine absence of settlement (Gibson 1992; Rowly-Conway 2000; Barclay 2001). Where palaeosols of Neolithic date, sealed beneath alluvium, have been examined, as is the case in parts of eastern England (*e.g.* French *et al.* 1992), the apparent absence of such settlements may indicate local adaptation and should not necessarily be extrapolated as being the case for other parts of Britain.

In conclusion, it is important that we remain receptive to new evidence. Within different parts of the region (and the rest of Britain) at any one time there may have been early Neolithic mobile foragers, early Neolithic mobile forager-farmers and early Neolithic sedentary farmers. Our aim now must be build into our research the accumulation of direct indicators rather than placing too much reliance on assumptions. Regions such as the East Midlands, with its successful agricultural history, may still hold many of the answers, but in less visible and less accessible forms than areas that have seen less agricultural exploitation over the last three millennia. However by using appropriate techniques the truth is still out there – but to get at it we must use more of the 'pitch'.

Bibliography

Ainsworth, S., 2001, Prehistoric settlement remains on the Derbyshire Gritstone Moors. *Derbyshire Archaeological Journal*, 121, 19–69.

Ainsworth, S. and Barnatt, J., 1998, A scarp-edge enclosure at Gardom's Edge Baslow, Derbyshire. *Derbyshire Archaeological Journal*, 118, 5–23.

Bamford, H, 1985, *Briar Hill, Northampton 1974–1978* (Northampton Development Corporation Monograph 3). Northampton. Northampton Development Corporation.

Barclay, G. J., 2001, 'Metropolitan' and 'parochial'/'core' and 'periphery': a historiography of the Neolithic of Scotland. *Proceedings of the Prehistoric Society*, 67, 1–18.

Barnatt, J., 1986, Bronze Age remains on the East Moors of the Peak District. *Derbyshire Archaeological Journal*, 106, 18–100.

Barnatt, J., 1987, Bronze Age settlement on the gritstone East Moors of the Peak District of Derbyshire and South Yorkshire. *Proceedings of the Prehistoric Society*, 53, 393–418.

Barnatt, J., 1990, *The Henges, Stone Circles and Ringcairns of the Peak District* (Sheffield Archaeological Monograph 1). Sheffield. University of Sheffield.

Barnatt, J., 1996, Moving beyond the Monuments: Paths and People in the Neolithic Landscapes of the Peak District. In P. Frodsham, (ed.), 1996, 43–59.

Barnatt, J. and Smith, K., 1997, *The Peak District: Landscapes through Time*. London: Batsford/ English Heritage.

Barnatt, J. and Thomas, G. H., 1998, Prehistoric Mining at Ecton, Staffordshire: a dated antler tool and its context. *Mining History*, 13.5, 72–78.

Barrett, J. C., 1994, *Fragments from Antiquity: The archaeology of social life in Britain 2900–1200BC*. Oxford. Blackwell.

Beamish, M., 2001, Excavations at Willington, south Derbyshire. Interim Report. *Derbyshire Archaeological Journal*, 121, 1–18.

Beamish, M. and Ripper, S., 2000, Burnt Mounds in the East Midlands. *Antiquity*, 75, 37–38.

Bird, A. J. and Bird, K. M., 1972, *A Prehistoric Hut-floor at Stanton-on-the-Wolds, Nottinghamshire. Transactions of the Thoroton Society*, 76, 4–12.

Bishop, M., 1999, *An archaeological resource assessment of the Neolithic and Bronze Age in Nottinghamshire. East Midlands Archaeological Research Frameworks*. www.le.ac.uk/archaeology/research/projects/eastmidsfw/pdfs/15nottneba.pdf

Bradley, P., 1989, A Leicestershire Source for Group XX. *Transactions of the Leicestershire Archaeological and Historical Society*, 68, 1–5.

Bradley, R. and Hart, C. R., 1983, Prehistoric settlement in the third and second millennia bc: a preliminary analysis in the light of recent fieldwork. *Proceedings of the Prehistoric Society*, 49, 177–193.

Brown, A. G., 2000, Floodplain Vegetation History: Clearings as Potential Ritual Spaces? In A. S. Fairbairn (ed.) 2000, 49–62.

Butler, A. and Thomas, J., 1999, Husbands Bosworth, Wheler Lodge Farm (SK 635 825). *Transactions of the Leicestershire Archaeological and Historical Society*, 73, 100.

Butler, A., Thomas, J. and Clay, P., 2002, A causewayed enclosure at Husbands Bosworth, Leicestershire. In G. Varndell and P. Topping (eds), *Enclosures in Neolithic Europe*. Oxford. Oxbow. 107–109.

Chapman, A., 1997, The excavation of Neolithic and Medieval mounds at Tansor Crossroads, Northamptonshire, 1995. *Northamptonshire Archaeology*, 27, 3–50.

Chowne, P., 1993, *The excavation of a Neolithic settlement at Tattershall Thorpe, Lincolnshire. Sleaford*. East Anglian Archaeology.

Chowne, P., 1994, The Bain Valley Survey. In M. Parker Pearson and R. Schadla Hall (eds), 27–32.

Clare, T., 1986, Towards a re-appraisal of henge monuments. *Proceedings of the Prehistoric Society*, 52, 281–331.

Clare, T., 1987, Towards a re-appraisal of henge monuments; origins, evolution and hierarchies. *Proceedings of the Prehistoric Society*, 53, 457–477.

Clay, P., 1981, *The excavation of two multi-phase barrows at Sproxton and Eaton, Leicestershire* (Leicestershire Museums Art Galleries and Records Service Archaeological Report No.2). Leicester. Leicestershire Museums Art Galleries and Records Service.

Clay, P., 1996, *The exploitation of the East Midlands Claylands in Later Prehistory. Aspects of settlement and land-use from the Mesolithic to the Iron Age*. Unpublished Ph.D. thesis. University of Leicester.

Clay, P., 1998, Neolithic-Earlier Bronze Age pit circles and their environs at Burley Road, Oakham, Rutland. *Proceedings of the Prehistoric Society*, 64, 293–330.

Clay, P., 1999, The Neolithic and Bronze Age of Leicestershire and Rutland. *Transactions of the Leicestershire Archaeological and Historical Society*, 73, 1–18.

Clay, P., 2002, *The Prehistory of the East Midlands Claylands*. Leicester. Leicester Archaeology Monograph 9.

Clay, P., 2006, The Neolithic and Early Bronze Age. In N. J. Cooper (ed.), *The Archaeology of the East Midlands. An Archaeological Resource Assessment and Research Agenda*. Leicester. Leicester Archaeology Monograph 13, 69–88.

Cooney, G., 1997, Images of settlement and landscape in the Neolithic. In P Topping (ed.), 23–32.

Evans, J. G., 1991, The Mollusca. In J. G. Evans and D. D. A. Simpson, Giants Hill 2 Long barrow, Skendleby, Lincolnshire. *Archaeologia*, 109, 1–45.

Fairbairn A. S., (ed.), 2000, *Plants in Neolithic Britain and Beyond* (Neolithic Studies Group Seminar Papers 5). Oxford. Oxbow.

Fairweather, A. D. and Ralston, I. B. M., 1993, The Neolithic timber hall at Balbridie, Grampion Region, Scotland. A preliminary note on dating and plant macrofossils. *Antiquity*, 67, 313–323.

Field, N., 1985, A Multi-phased Barrow and possible Henge Monument at West Ashby, Lincolnshire. *Proceedings of the Prehistoric Society*, 51, 103–136.

French, C. A. I., 1991, *Excavations in advance of the A605 Bypass at Elton*. Northamptonshire Archaeology, 23, 79–82.

French, C. A. I., Macklin, M. G. and Passmore, D. G., 1992, Archaeology and palaeochannels in the lower Welland and Nene Valleys: alluvial archaeology at the fen-edge, eastern England. In S. Needham, and M. G. Macklin (eds), 1992, *Alluvial Archaeology in Britain*. Oxford. Oxbow. 169–176.

Foard, G. R., 1979, *Archaeological Priorities: Proposals for Northamptonshire* (Northamptonshire County Council Archaeology Occasional Paper 4). Northampton. Northamptonshire County Council.

Ford, S., 1987, *East Berkshire Archaeological Survey* (Berkshire County Council Occasional Paper No.1). Reading. Department of Highways and Planning.

Frodsham, P., (ed.), 1996, *Neolithic Studies in No-Mans land. Papers on the Neolithic of Northern England from the Trent to the Tweed*. (Northern Archaeology, 13/14 (special edition)). Newcastle. Northern Archaeology Group.

Gaffney, V. and Tingle, M., 1989, *The Maddle Farm Project – an integrated survey of prehistoric and rural landscapes on the Berkshire Downs* (BAR British Series 200). Oxford. British Archaeological Reports.

Garton, D., 1991, Neolithic settlement in the Peak District: Perspective and Prospects. In R Hodges and K Smith (eds), *Recent Developments in the Archaeology of the Peak District. Sheffield. University of Sheffield*. 3–21.

Garton, D., 1995, *Archaeological assessment of the proposed development area at Sherwood Park, Blackwell, Derbyshire*. Unpublished report. Matlock DCC archaeological reports archive.

Garton, D. and Beswick, P., 1983, The survey and excavation of a Neolithic settlement area at Mount Pleasant, Kenslow, 1980–1983. *Derbyshire Archaeological Journal*, 103, 7–40.

Garton, D. and Beswick, P, forthcoming, *A reassessment of the artefacts from the excavations within the enclosure at Swine Sty, Big Moor, Baslow with special reference to the pottery and flintwork*.

Garton, D. and Elliott, L., 1998, Acre Lane, Aston Upon Trent. *Derbyshire Archaeological Journal*, 118, 148–150.

Garton, D., Phillips, P. and Henson, D., 1989, Newton Cliffs: a flint working and settlement site in the Trent valley. In P. Phillips (ed.), 1989, 81–180.

Gibson, A., (ed.), 1989, *Midlands Prehistory* (BAR British Series 204). Oxford. British Archaeological Reports.

Gibson, A., 1992, Approaches to the later Neolithic and Bronze Age settlement of Britain. *Colloque interntional de lons-le-Saumier 16–19 mai 1990*, 41–48.

Gibson, A., 1994, Excavations at Sarn-y-Bryn-caled Cursus Complex, Welshpool, Powys and the timber circles of Great Britain and Ireland. *Proceedings of the Prehistoric Society*, 60, 143–224.

Gibson, A. and Loveday, R., 1989, *Excavations at the cursus monument of Aston upon Trent, Derbyshire*. In A. Gibson (ed.), 27–50.

Hall, D. N., 1985, Survey work in Eastern England. In S. Macready and F. H. Thompson (eds), *Archaeological Field Survey in Britain and Abroad* (Society of Antiquities Occasional Paper 6). London. Society of Antiquities. 25–44.

Harding, A. F. with Lee, G. E., 1987, *Henge Monuments and Related Sites of Great Britain* (BAR British Series 175). Oxford. British Archaeological Reports.

Harding, J., 1995, Social histories and regional perspectives in the Neolithic of lowland Britain. *Proceedings of the Prehistoric Society*, 61, 117–136.

Hart, C. R., 1985, Aleck Low and Upper House Farm, Derbyshire: Prehistoric artefact scatters. In D. Spratt and C. Burgess (eds), 51–69.

Hawke-Smith, C. F., 1979, *Man-Land Relations in Prehistoric Britain: the Dove Derwent Interfluve* (BAR British Series 64). Oxford. British Archaeological Reports.

Hawkes, C. F. C., 1932, The Towednack Gold Hoard. *Man*, 32, 177–186.

Hayes, P. P. and Lane T., 1992, *Lincolnshire Survey. The South-West Fens, Sleaford.* East Anglian Archaeology.

Hey, G., 1997, Neolithic settlement at Yarnton, Oxfordshire. In P. Topping (ed.), 99–112.

Hicks, S. P., 1971, Pollen analytical evidence for the effect of prehistoric agriculture on the vegetation of N. Derbyshire. *New Phytologist*, 70, 647–667.

Hicks, S. P., 1972, The impact of man on the East Moor of Derbyshire from Mesolithic times. *Archaeological Journal*, 129, 1–21.

Hughes, G. and Rosseff, R., 1995, Excavations at Croft Quarry (SP 517 968). *Transactions of the Leicestershire Archaeological and Historical Society*, 69, 100–108.

Jones, D., 1998, Long barrows and elongated enclosures in Lincolnshire: An analysis of the Air Photographic evidence. *Proceedings of the Prehistoric Society*, 64, 83–114.

Jones, G., 2000, Evaluating the importance of cultivation and collecting in Neolithic Britain. In A. S. Fairbairn (ed.), 79–84.

Keevill, G., 1992, Life on the edge: archaeology and alluvium at Redlands Farm, Stanwick, Northants. In S. Needham and M. G. Macklin (eds), 177–184.

Kidd, S., 1999, *The 1st Millennium BC in Northamptonshire: A Resource Assessment. The East Midlands Archaeological Research Frameworks Project Stage 1: An Archaeological Resource Assessment.*

Knight, D., 1999, The Derby Southern by-pass. *Current Archaeology*, 157, 32–33.

Lane, T., 1993, *Lincolnshire Survey. The Northern Fen Edge.* Sleaford. East Anglian Archaeology.

Liddle, P., 1985, *Community Archaeology: A Fieldworkers Handbook of Organisation and Techniques.* Leicester. Leicestershire Museums, Art Galleries and Records Service.

Liddle, P., 1994, The Medbourne Area Survey. In M. Parker Pearson and R. T. Schadla-Hall (eds), 34–36.

Loveday, R., 2004, Contextualising monuments – the exceptional potential of the middle Trent valley. *Derbyshire Archaeological Journal*, 124, 1–12.

Makepeace, G. A., 1999, Cratcliff Rocks: a forgotten hillfort. *Derbyshire Archaeological Journal*, 119, 12–18.

May, J., 1976, *Prehistoric Lincolnshire* (History of Lincolnshire 1). Lincoln. History of Lincolnshire Committee.

McCullagh, P., 1969, *The East Midlands. A Regional Study.* Oxford. Oxford University Press.

Mills, N. W. T., 1985, Sample bias, regional analysis and fieldwalking in British archaeology. In C. Haselgrove, M. Millett and I. Smith (eds), *Archaeology from the ploughsoil. Studies in the collection and interpretation of Field Survey data.* Sheffield. University of Sheffield Department of Archaeology and Prehistory. 39–47.

Mithen, S. J., 1990, *Thoughtful Foragers: a Study in Prehistoric Decision Making.* Cambridge. Cambridge University Press.

Moore, W. R. G. and Williams, J. H., 1975, A Later Neolithic site at Ecton, Northampton. *Northamptonshire Archaeology*, 10, 3–30.

Myers, A. M., 1991, *The North Derbyshire transect survey: preliminary assessment of the lithic evidence.* Unpublished report. Bakewell, PDNPA archaeological archive.

Oswald, A., Dyer, C. and Barber, M., 2001, *The Creation of Monuments. Neolithic Causewayed Enclosures in the British Isles.* Swindon. English Heritage.

Palmer, R., 1976, Interrupted Ditch Enclosures in Britain: the use of Aerial Photography for Comparative Studies. *Proceedings of the Prehistoric Society*, 46, 161–186.

Parker Pearson, M. and Schadla-Hall, R. T., (eds), 1994, *Looking at the Land. Archaeological*

Landscapes in Eastern England. Recent Work and Future Directions. Leicester. Leicestershire Museums, Art Galleries and Records Service.

Parry, S. J., 1994, The Raunds Area Project Survey. In M. Parker Pearson and R. T. Schadla-Hall (eds), 36–42.

Parry, S. J., 2005, *The Raunds Area Survey. An archaeological study of the landscape of Raunds, Northamptonshire 1985–92*. Oxford. Oxbow/English Heritage.

Philips C. W., 1935, Neolithic 'A' bowl from near Grantham. *Antiquaries Journal*, 15, 347–348.

Phillips, P., (ed.), 1989, *Archaeology and Landscape Studies in North Lincolnshire* (BAR British Series 208 i and ii). Oxford. British Archaeological Reports.

Pickering, J., 1989, Discovering the Prehistoric Midlands. In A Gibson (ed.), 106–110.

Pickering, J. and Hartley, R. F., 1985, *Past Worlds in a Landscape*. Leicester. Leicestershire Museums, Art Galleries and Records Service.

RCHME, 1975, *An Inventory of the Historical Monuments in the County of Northampton; Volume I, Archaeological Sites in North-East Northamptonshire*. London. Royal Commission on Historical Monuments, England.

RCHME, 1985, *An Inventory of the Historical Monuments in the County of Northampton; Volume V, Archaeological Sites and Churches in Northampton*. London. Royal Commission on Historical Monuments, England.

Radley, J. and Cooper, L. B., 1968, A Neolithic site at Elton: an experiment in field recording. *Derbyshire Archaeological Journal*, 88, 37–46.

Reaney, D., 1968, Beaker burials in South Derbyshire. *Derbyshire Archaeological Journal*, 88, 68–81.

Rowley-Conwy, P., 2000, Through a taphonomic glass, darkly: the importance of cereal production in prehistoric Britain. In J. P. Huntley and S. Stallibrass (eds), *Taphonomy and Interpretation* (Symposia of the Association for Environmental Archaeology No.14). Oxford. Oxbow. 43–53.

Scaife, R. G. and Allen, M. J., 1999, A Prehistoric Vegetational History from the Trent Valley, near Cottam, Nottinghamshire. *Transactions of the Thoroton Society of Nottinghamshire*, 10, 315–24.

Schulting, R. J., 2000, New AMS dates from the Lambourn long barrow and the question of the earliest Neolithic in southern England: repacking the Neolithic package? *Oxford Journal of Archaeology*, 19.1, 25–35.

Taylor, D. M., Griffiths, H. I., Pedley, H. M. and Prince, I., 1994, Radiocarbon-dated Holocene pollen and ostracod sequences from barrage tufa-dammed fluvial systems in the White Peak, Derbyshire UK. *The Holocene*, 4, 356–364.

Thomas, J., 1996, Neolithic houses in mainland Britain and Ireland – a sceptical view. In T. Darvill and J. Thomas (eds), *Neolithic Houses in northwest Europe and beyond* (Neolithic Studies Group Seminar Papers 6). Oxford. Oxbow. 1–12.

Topping, P., (ed.), 1997, *Neolithic Landscapes* (Neolithic Studies Group Seminar Papers 2). Oxford. Oxbow.

Vine, P. M., 1982, *The Neolithic and Bronze Age Cultures of the Middle and Upper Trent Basin* (BAR British Series 105). Oxford. British Archaeological Reports.

Wheeler, H., 1970, The Findern Cursus. *Derbyshire Archaeological Journal*, 90, 4–7.

Wheeler, H., 1979, Excavation at Willington, Derbyshire 1970–1972. *Derbyshire Archaeological Journal*, 99, 58–220.

Whittle, A. W. R., 1997, Moving on and moving around: Neolithic settlement mobility. In P. Topping (ed.), 15–22.

Wilson, D. M., 1975, Causewayed camps and interrupted ditch systems. *Antiquity*, 49, 178–186.

Wiltshire, P. E. J. and Edwards, K. J., 1993, Mesolithic, early Neolithic and later prehistoric impacts on vegetation at a riverine site in Derbyshire, England. In F M. Chambers (ed.), *Climate Change and Human Impact on the Landscape*. London: Chapman and Hall. 157–168.

Windell, D., 1989, A Later Neolithic 'Ritual Focus' at West Cotton, Northamptonshire. In A. Gibson (ed.), 85–94.

Chapter 9

The role of islands in defining identity and regionality during the Neolithic: the Dublin coastal group

Gabriel Cooney

INTRODUCTION

Islands are very often invoked as critically important places in looking at issues of identity and regionality. The concept of islands as physically bounded worlds, ideal as small-scale laboratories for the study of cultural process, is an idea that has been current in archaeological research since Evans' (1973) influential paper. But there are different ways of thinking about islands, as seen as in the development of island archaeology in the Pacific (*e.g.* Terrell 1986; Gosden and Pavlides 1994) and in the Mediterranean (*e.g.* Patton 1996; Broodbank 2000; Robb 2001). In his book, *An Island Archaeology of the Early Cyclades* (2000), Broodbank suggests that if we rethink some of the basic assumptions that have traditionally informed much archaeological research about islands, the way can be opened to a more culturally nuanced island archaeology. He argues that we need to recognise the extent to which islanders consciously fashion and refashion their own identities and worlds. This also involves getting away from the concept of individual islands as units for analysing island societies. Instead we have to think about connections and linkages between islands and mainlands – islandscapes. Following on from this and from the wider recognition of the active social role of things, island material culture has to be seen as having an active, participatory role in island life. It offers us the opportunity to explore inter-island and island-mainland relationships.

My interest in this approach comes from a research programme on a small island in the Irish Sea, Lambay, off the east coast of Ireland to the north of Dublin. Fieldwork has been dominated by an excavation project that started off as a small test excavation of a Neolithic quarry site, called the Eagle's Nest (Cooney 1998; 2000). But increasingly over time we have been drawn into trying to understand the long-term human history of the island. More pertinent to the excavation, which has been completed (Cooney 2002a), the activities and events reflected in the material culture made it clear that the site had to be placed in a wider spatial and cultural context. Standing at the site, which is located centrally on relatively high ground, and looking round one is immediately aware that Lambay as an island cannot be understood in isolation from its geographical context. It forms part of an island group off the Dublin coastline (Figure 9.1) whose importance we have perhaps underestimated in understanding prehistoric societies in this part of the Irish Sea zone. From north to south this group consists of four small islands near the town of Skerries (Colt Island, Saint Patrick's Island, Shenick's Island close to the shore and Rockabill further out), Lambay Island, Ireland's Eye, Howth (today a peninsula, probably an island in the

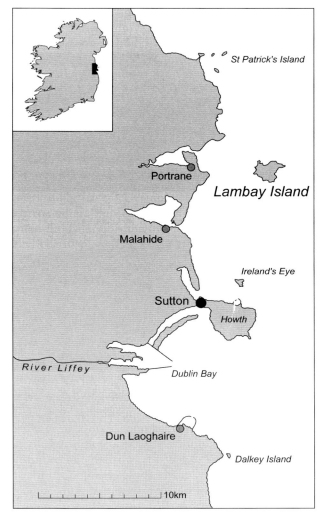

Figure 9.1 The location of the islands off the Dublin coastline.

early Neolithic) and Dalkey Island. On three of these islands, Dalkey, Howth and Lambay, there is important evidence for Neolithic activity that will be explored below. But it might be useful to begin by considering more broadly the role of islands in the Neolithic.

SEEING NEOLITHIC ISLANDS

What was the attraction and importance of islands in the Neolithic of this part of north-west Europe? It is relevant to remind ourselves how frequently archaeologists suggest that the concept of an island and insularity was understood by Neolithic people. As well as actual islands we discuss the significance of places that are 'almost' islands, such as Knockadoon at Lough Gur, Co. Limerick (Ó Ríordáin 1954; Grogan and Eogan 1987). It is only a short conceptual step to giving quasi-island status to islands with a distinct physical character, where, as Broodbank (2000, 16) puts it, spaces are surrounded by something else (other than, or only partially by, water). One example would be Brú na Bóinne (the Bend of the Boyne) in eastern Ireland (Mitchell 1984; Cooney 2000). Robb (2001, 196) uses the term 'cultural islands' to describe a context in small-scale, traditional societies where a geographical area shows a recombination and elaboration of cultural elements from broader regions with fuzzy cultural boundaries allied to unique local cultural expression. Interestingly, he makes the point that these cultural islands share a general common size.

Islands are also metaphors for space in which the relationship between people and the material world can be established and recorded (Papastergiadis 1998). Hence, for Neolithic societies we suggest that part of the idea of enclosure is about the concept of creating bounded worlds (*e.g.* Edmonds 1993). It has been argued that in some instances in making monuments people are representing their world as an island. Relevant examples include the suggestion that on the main island (Mainland) of Orkney, off the coast of northern Scotland, henges are a microcosm of the Orcadian island world (Richards 1996) and Tilley's (1999) discussion of the Maiden Castle Neolithic complex in southern England as a representation of the Isle of Portland on the coast to the south.

Taking a historical perspective it might be useful to consider the extent to which areas of Neolithic settlement, and the movement of ideas and material between them, might at least initially (late Mesolithic/early Neolithic) have been perceived and had the physical characteristics of islands or enclaves within what was still by and large a woodland world. Movement by inland waterways and along coasts may have been the vital communication connection between such areas. One possible framework for examining change during the Neolithic (middle and late) is in terms of the expansion and shifting boundaries of these 'islands'. Looking back, Tilley (1999, 197) has suggested that in the Neolithic of southern England the ideology of the island as a place of ancestral origins may have been widespread, reflected for example in the choice of hilltop 'islands' for enclosures. If the concept of an island cultural origin was common, we could interpret this is a number of ways. One would be to suggest that it evokes a sense of continuity from the Mesolithic. To support this view we can recall the very strong evidence for the use of islands in the Mesolithic. As McCartan (2000) has pointed out in the Irish Mesolithic both lake islands (see O'Sullivan 1998) and coastal islands of varying size were in use for a variety of purposes. Alternatively we could situate the notion of island origins in the movement of people, along the Atlantic coast for enclave colonisation (Zilhão 1993, 2000). Enclave colonisation is defined as island or area hopping, involving the small-scale movement of people with a strong maritime, island tradition. Sheridan (2000) has posited such a scenario to explain early Neolithic connections between western France and western Scotland.

We should of course bear in mind the danger of archaeological interpretation of islands being influenced by 'island discourse' in which islands are often portrayed, both in colonial literature and postmodern society, as remote venues for adventure, awaiting discovery, description and control, the ideal counter-points to home (*e.g.* Papastergiadis 1998). However, there is very strong support for the view that in many societies, past and present, islands were perceived as having cosmological or religious significance. For example, in early medieval Ireland the otherworld was often portrayed as an island, or as a series of disparate islands (*e.g.* Mac Cana 1976). The significance of islands may have lain in their role as one of a number of types of natural places; others being caves, mountains, springs and rivers, which were seen as liminal but linking, dangerous but powerful because of their spatial location (Bradley 2000). In this context, Helms (1988, 25) has made the important point that islands have a particular character as sacred, special places because they are where the land, the sea and the sky meet. Hence two liminal zones are created; at the junction of the land and the sea (coast) and the land and the sky over the island. One might be initially inclined to think of physically remote islands as the ones that would have been regarded as of special power and significance. However if we accept that just as vertical space may be cosmologically charged, so might horizontal distance (*ibid.*, 4), then physical distance between islands and mainland becomes much less relevant. Because of their special character islands, even those spatially close to the mainland, may have had a special role. The activities that took place there may have been may have been imbued with a particular character, as has been argued to be the case with crannogs, the artificial lake islands of early medieval Ireland (O'Sullivan forthcoming).

THE DUBLIN COAST LANDSCAPE

The last point is relevant to the particular group of islands that I wish to discuss here, those off, but relatively close to, the coast of Dublin. Apart from considering the special roles that these islands may have had because they were islands, they may also have had an important economic role as a source of food or other resources (McCartan 2000). Again the question arises as to whether these resources might have been seen as 'special' because of their island origin.

Given the location of this island group it is also worth bearing in mind their potential significance in the early medieval and medieval period as contact points in the network of linkage and exchange between the larger islands (mainlands) of Britain and Ireland (*e.g.* Wooding 1996; Doyle 1998; Breen 2001). If they served as contact points for exchange and trade across the Irish Sea in prehistory, evoking Helms again (1988, 13) it is tempting to see these islands as having a role in mediating contact between distant places. The ideological aura that may have surrounded such material, carrying with it knowledge of distant realms and regions, could have been the basis for the spread of ideas and information. Possession of such material, coming locally from these special islands, may have been regarded as signifying power and knowledge. In this regard the strategic position of the islands in terms of travel across and along the western side of the Irish Sea cannot be downplayed. The pattern of currents in the Irish Sea makes it easier to travel along coasts (Waddell 1991/2) and these islands, especially Lambay, form dramatic markers on the horizon as one approaches the mainland coast. Locally, the islands are ideal places from which to monitor and if necessary control the movement of boats along this strip of the eastern coastline of Ireland.

So what about the archaeological evidence on these islands that could back up the suggestion that they were regarded as special places? Bradley (2000, 36) has argued that there are a number of ways in which we could demonstrate the significance of particular natural places; the deliberate deposition of material, the embellishment of striking features of the landscape with monuments (or 'art') and the deployment of objects made at and from these special places. In this first look at the Dublin island group I want to say something briefly about Howth and Dalkey and to dwell a little longer on Lambay.

HOWTH AS AN ISLAND

Howth today forms a peninsula framing the north side of Dublin. It is linked to the mainland by a narrow tombolo. In earlier prehistory, Howth was an island (Figure 9.2) about 2.5km off the coast and about 700ha in area (McCartan 2000, 19). Mitchell (1956, 1972) excavated a midden on the west side of the island. There are now three dates from the excavation that span the period 7000–5000BP (Woodman *et al.* 1997, 144). This suggests that the site should be discussed as a focus in the local pattern of late Mesolithic activity rather than just in the context of the Mesolithic/Neolithic transition as has been the case. There is a portal tomb (Ó Nualláin 1983) located to the east of a cliff face and three small hilltop cairns. There is an interesting question here about the relationship between the portal tomb and the stage at which Howth became linked to the mainland. If the monument was constructed when Howth was still an island, then its significance as the only portal tomb in the Dublin group on the mainland north of the River Liffey (see Cooney 2000) is enhanced. It would also indicate that the special character of this island was marked by the construction of a type

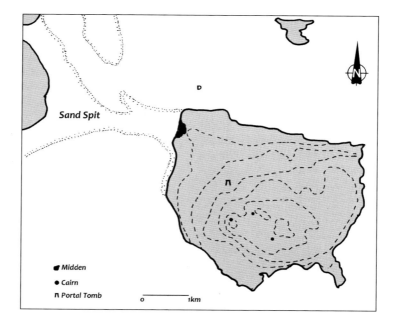

Figure 9.2 Howth as an island in the late Mesolithic and Neolithic. (Contours at 10m intervals).

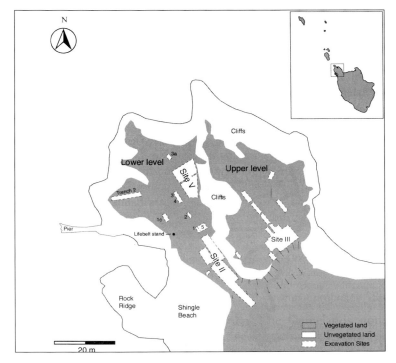

Figure 9.3 Dalkey island, with the location of Liversage's (1968) site V and SMG II.

of megalithic tomb that occurs not just in Dublin but also in coastal areas on both sides of the Irish Sea (Ó Nualláin 1983; Mercer 1986; Lynch 1989, 2000).

DALKEY ISLANDS – ACROSS THE SOUND

Dalkey is a small island that forms the southernmost of the group of islands off the Dublin coast (Figures 9.1 and 9.3). It lies about 400m offshore, separated from the mainland by a deep sound with strong tidal currents. It is only about 7ha in extent and certainly justifies the title of a small island. Dalkey Island is perhaps best known for the Mesolithic evidence recovered during the excavation of a promontory fort at the northern end of the island in the 1950s (Site II and V) where at the base of the stratigraphic sequence midden deposits and associated activities were uncovered. The initial radiocarbon dated and stratigraphic evidence suggested that this was a site that was relevant to understanding the Mesolithic/ Neolithic transition and it has frequently been discussed in this regard. Dating of mammal bone by the Irish Quaternary Faunas Project (Woodman *et al.* 1997) has pushed the dating of the beginning of the use of the site back to 7250BP (before 6000BC) and indicates that it had a much longer-term pattern of usage than had previously been thought (Woodman 2000, 228). The site has been written about primarily in economic terms (Liversage 1968;

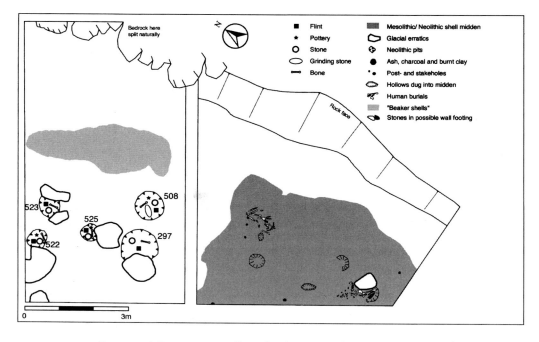

Figure 9.4 Features at Dalkey island, site V (after Liversage 1968).

McCartan 2000) but re-examination of the stone axeheads and associated material from the site by Leon (2001) suggests that it is open to a different interpretation (Figure 9.4).

It is clear firstly that activity also went on for much of the duration of the Neolithic. For example, some of the stone axeheads can definitely be said to be Neolithic in date because of their association with Neolithic ceramics. From the presence of grinding slabs it appears that in the Neolithic axeheads could have been produced on the island from beach cobbles, coming from sources on the shore at the north end of the island or from the mainland beaches further to the south. Alternatively both axes and grinding stones may have been brought to be deposited on the island. There is a series of features post-dating and in some cases dug into the middens that Liversage interpreted as domestic but which contain deliberate deposits and in some cases appear to mark or be marked by boulders. There is at least one definite Neolithic burial associated with the shell midden at Site II and Liversage suggested that the two burials at Site V may pre-date the deposition of Beaker pottery and associated activity (1968, 63, 103). It begins to look as if a range of material is being brought to Dalkey and then deliberately deposited there. This is a pattern of activity that may well have started in the Mesolithic as it seems unlikely that wild pig, one of the main mammals represented in the faunal remains, or other animals such as bear (represented by phalanges, see Hatting 1968) would have lived on the island. In this regard the location of the site on the island should be noted (see Figure 9.3). It is at the base of a low cliff, overlooked by higher ground and overlooking the sound with a view across to the mainland. This pattern of episodic deposition seems to have continued to the end of the Neolithic, as there are sherds from late Neolithic ceramics and Beaker on Dalkey (Liversage 1968; Clarke 1970; Sheridan 1995). (The attraction of an accessible off-shore island like Dalkey as a venue for ceremonial events is echoed in recent times by the annual public festival held on the island during the eighteenth century to mark the election of the 'king of Dalkey' (Fewer 1998).)

LAMBAY – LANDMARKS AND LOCAL IDENTITY

About 11km north of Howth and 8km from the nearest part of the Dublin coastline, Lambay has a dramatic skyline, a consequence of its largely volcanic origins (Stillman 1994), enhanced by a large cairn on the highest point of the island, Knockbane (the white cairn). There is little by way of known Mesolithic material although there is a late Mesolithic artefact in the Keillor-Knowles collection (Finlay and Woodman, pers. comm.; see also Mitchell 1990, 48). A Neolithic site was uncovered on the harbour close to the west side of the island in the 1920s (Macalister 1929). Excavation has been completed of a Neolithic axe quarry site at the Eagle's Nest close to centre of the island (*e.g.* Cooney 1998, 2000, 2002a, 2002b). There is clear evidence on the site for material culture and events in the Neolithic that seem both to evoke the particular character of Lambay as an island but that also link that to a wider world. Examining such evidence one is reminded of Brookbank's (2000, 363) description of island people as people who are neither entirely different from the rest of the world nor yet wholly similar.

At the Eagle's Nest site a distinctive medium-grained volcanic rock, porphyry, or porphyritic andesite, was exploited for the production of stone axeheads. The primary process of production was by hammering and pecking followed by grinding. All stages of axe production took place at the site. There is evidence of quarrying in the middle/late Neolithic, but perhaps including a phase in the early Neolithic, and also of deliberate deposition, both in the quarry areas and the floor of a small valley between two worked outcrops (Figure 9.5). On this valley floor there is a sequence of features that appear to begin with pits, some of which appear tohave been deliberately cut into by later pits. Then there is a switch to the placing on the ground of features and a range of cultural material, for example a hoard of objects including a pestle macehead and also a porphyry roughout and axe. Some of the contemporary features are reminiscent of the settings outside passage tombs. One of the notable features of the material culture is the deposition of jasper; broken and tested pebbles and a small number of beads and pendants, the latter a type that are typically found in deposits in passage tombs (*e.g.* Eogan 1986). The evidence suggests that jasper from outcrop veins and beach pebbles was being worked, either at the site or elsewhere on the island. Deposits of beach gravel at the site are another indicator of the deliberate placement of material brought up from the coast. Ultimately, this build-up of material resulted in the creation of a low cairn, a maximum of about 10m in diameter.

At the moment it is attractive to think of the Eagle's Nest site as a place where porphyry was worked and deposited and where other material was brought and deposited. In these actions the connections between a range of material culture, and the people involved, were reworked. The placement of material on or under the ground may have been viewed as

Figure 9.5 Activities at the Eagle's Nest site, Lambay: (left) quarrying of porphyritic andesite (porphyry) outcrops; (right) deposition of material in pits and on the ground surface.

making linkages through a powerful conduit to the realm of the supernatural (La Motta and Schiffer 2001). In the deposition of porphyry axes and roughouts we see the beginning and the end of the biographical cycle of objects happening in the same location. Going back to Bradley's (2000) test of the significance of natural places, his three major signifiers occur at this site: distinctive deposits, the embellishment of the landscape and artefacts made at special locations.

Moving away from the Eagle's Nest site it is worth noting that there are quarried porphyry pieces in the makeup of the cairn at Knockbane, the most notable prehistoric landmark on the island. Knockbane also takes us out to the wider world, it is placed to be seen (Figure 9.6). It is noteworthy that the profile of Lambay viewed from the west resembles the shape of the most striking of the peaks in the Wicklow mountains on the mainland, namely the Sugerloaf, as seen from Lambay. From the island it seems to emerge from the top of Howth. Looking north from Knockbane there is a distant view to Slieve Gullion (with two passage tombs on the summit) and the Carlingford and Mourne mountains (including Slieve Donard with the highest hilltop passage tomb in Ireland). Given these kinds of links it is obvious that the Neolithic activities on Lambay cannot be seen in isolation. What we are seeing are the links between activities on a specific island and the wider cultural setting in which they took place. Cunliffe (2001) has used the Boyne-Orcadian axis for this wider cultural setting in the middle and late Neolithic (see also discussion in Cooney 2000, 224–8). As a specific example the pestle-type maceheads (and there are fragments of others) from the Eagle's Nest site can be compared with those found in settlement and tomb contexts in Orkney and with the only example found in a secure archaeological context in Ireland, from outside the outer sill-stone in the passage of the western tomb

Figure 9.6 (top) Looking south from Lambay, the top of Sugarloaf mountain appearing from over the Howth peninsula; (bottom) Lambay from the west, the Knockbane cairn prominent as the highest point on the island.

structure under the main mound at Knowth (Simpson and Ransom 1992, 227). What we have at the Eagle's Nest site is the material manifestation of what Robb (2001, 196) has called the 'reworking of a regional symbolic heritage into a local, cosmologically grounded identity'. The special contribution that Lambay may have made to the regional symbolic world is in the small number of porphyry axes from Lambay that have been recognised on the mainland of Ireland (and perhaps jasper ornaments, although this research issue has still to be addressed). That the island of Lambay was involved in other webs of connection across the Irish Sea is indicated by the recognition that the axeheads from the site close to the harbour discovered in the 1920s have their closest geochemical match in the Group XIII axes from south-west Wales (Cooney and Mandal 1995).

CONCLUSION

Much of what has been said here should be taken as a first attempt at an understanding of what is a significant group of islands during the Neolithic. While the importance of individual islands off the Dublin coastline has been noted in the past, the fact that as a group they give a particular character to this part of the Irish Sea littoral has not. The long-term significance of these islands for people on the mainland of Ireland has also been underplayed. It may be coincidental but it is worth noting that in the case of Howth, Dalkey and Lambay there is definite activity and some sense of a focus on the side of the islands facing across to the mainland during the Mesolithic and Neolithic. There are certainly strong indications that these islands were regarded as special places during the Neolithic. They played a role as places that could be both distant in a sacred sense and local in a physical sense. On the other hand there are indications that they were linked into a wider world of Irish Sea-based contacts. In coastal areas the sea is the means of contact. Perhaps as Raban (2000) has so eloquently suggested for the Pacific coast of north-west America it is the key to understanding the life and culture of the people who inhabit its dry edges but who live across its fluid surface.

ACKNOWLEDGEMENTS

My thanks to Barbara Leon and Emmett O'Keeffe for the line drawings and to Rob Sands for his work on the photographs. I am very grateful to Barbara Leon and Aidan O'Sullivan for their comments from which the paper has greatly benefited.

Bibliography

Bradley, R., 2000, *An archaeology of natural places*. London. Routledge.

Breen, C., 2001, The maritime cultural landscape in medieval Gaelic Ireland. In P. J. Duffy, D. Edwards and E. Fitzpatrick (eds), *Gaelic Ireland: land, lordship and settlement c.1250–c.1650*. Dublin. Four Courts Press. 418–435.

Broodbank, C., 2000, *An island archaeology of the early Cyclades*. Cambridge. Cambridge University Press.

Clarke, D. L., 1970, *Beaker pottery of Great Britain and Ireland*. Cambridge. Cambridge University Press.

Cooney, G., 1998, Breaking stones, making places. In A. Gibson and D. D. A. Simpson (eds), *Prehistoric ritual and religion*. Stroud. Sutton Publishing. 108–118.

Cooney, G., 2000, *Landscapes of Neolithic Ireland*. London. Routledge.

Cooney, G., 2002a, Lambay Island: Neolithic axe production and associated activity. In I. Bennett (ed.), *Excavations 2000*. Bray. Wordwell.

Cooney, G., 2002b, So many shades of rock: colour symbolism in Irish stone axeheads. In A. Jones and G. MacGregor (eds), *Colouring the past*. London. Berg. 93–107.

Cooney, G. and Mandal, S., 1995, Getting to the core of the problem: petrological results from the Irish Stone Axe Project. *Antiquity*, 69, 969–980.

Cunliffe, B., 2001, *Facing the ocean: the Atlantic and its peoples*. Oxford. Oxford University Press.

Doyle, I., 1998, The early medieval activity at Dalkey island, Co. Dublin: a re-assessment. *Journal of Irish Archaeology*, 9, 89–104.

Edmonds, M., 1993, Interpreting causewayed enclosures in the present and the past. In C. Tilley (ed.), *Intepretative archaeology*. Oxford. Berg. 99–142.

Eogan, G., 1986, *Knowth and the passage tombs of Ireland*. London. Thames and Hudson.

Evans, J. D., 1973, Islands as laboratories for the study of culture process. In A. C. Renfrew (ed.), *The explanation of culture change: models in prehistory*. London. Duckworth. 517–520.

Fewer, M., 1998, *By swerve of shore: exploring Dublin's coast*. Dublin. Gill and Macmillan.

Gosden, C. and Pavlides., C, 1994, Are islands insular? Landscape vs. seascape in the case of the Arawe islands, Papua New Guinea. *Archaeology in Oceania*, 29, 162–171.

Grogan, E. and Eogan, G., 1987, Lough Gur excavations by Sean P. O'Ríordain: further Neolithic and Beaker habitations on Knockdoon. *Proceedings of the Royal Irish Academy*, 87C, 299–506.

Hatting, T., 1968, Animal bones from the basal middens. In G. D. Liversage, *Excavations at Dalkey island, Co. Dublin, 1956–1959*. Proceedings of the Royal Irish Academy, 66C, 172–174.

Helms, M. W., 1988, *Ulysses' sail: an ethnographic odyssey of power, knowledge and geographical distance*. Princeton. Princeton University Press.

La Motta, V. M. and Schiffer, M. B., 2001, Behavioural archaeology: towards a new synthesis. In I. Hodder (ed.), *Archaeological theory today*. Cambridge. Polity Press.

Leon, B., 2001, *A reassessment of stone axeheads from Dalkey island, Co. Dublin*. Unpublished MA thesis, University College Dublin.

Liversage, G. D., 1968, *Excavations at Dalkey island, Co. Dublin, 1956–1959*. Proceedings of the Royal Irish Academy, 66C, 53–233.

Lynch, F., 1989, Wales and Ireland in prehistory: a fluctuating relationship. *Archaeologia Cambrensis*, 138, 1–19.

Lynch, F., 2000, The earlier Neolithic. In F. Lynch, S. Aldhouse-Green and J. L. Davies (eds), *Prehistoric Wales*. Stroud. Sutton. 42–78.

Macalister, R. A. S., 1929, On some antiquities discovered upon Lambay island. *Proceedings of the Royal Irish Academy*, 38C, 240–246.

McCartan, S., 2000, The utilisation of island environments in the Irish Mesolithic: agendas for Rathlin island. In A. Desmond, G. Johnson, M. McCarthy, J. Sheehan and E. Shee Twohig (eds), *New agendas in Irish prehistory*. Bray. Wordwell. 15–30.

Mac Cana, P., 1976, The sinless otherworld of Immran Brain. *Eriu*, 27, 95–115.

Mercer, R., 1986, The Neolithic in Cornwall. *Cornish Archaeology*, 25, 35–80.

Mitchell, G. F., 1956, An early kitchen-midden at Sutton, Co. Dublin. *Journal of the Royal Society of Antiquaries of Ireland*, 86, 1–26.

Mitchell, G. F., 1972, Further Excavations of the Early Kitchen-Midden at Sutton, Co. Dublin. *Journal of the Royal Society of Antiquaries of Ireland* 102, 151–159.

Mitchell, G. F., 1984, The landscape. In G. Eogan, *Excavations at Knowth 1. Dublin*. Royal Irish Academy. 9–11.

Mitchell, G. F., 1990, *The way that I followed: a naturalist's journey across Ireland*. Dublin. Country House.

Ó Nualláin, S., 1983, Irish portal tombs: topography, siting and distribution, *Journal of the Royal Society of Antiquaries of Ireland*, 113, 75–105.

O'Sullivan, A., 1998, *The archaeology of lake settlement in Ireland* (Discovery Programme Monograph 4). Dublin. Discovery Programme and Royal Irish Academy.

O'Sullivan, A., forthcoming, *Fortunate isles: interpreting crannogs in early medieval Ireland* (Paper presented at the 'Wetland landscapes and cultural responses' conference, British Academy, London, 2001).

Ó Ríordáin, S. P., 1954, Lough Gur excavations: Neolithic and Bronze Age houses on Knockadoon. *Proceedings of the Royal Irish Academy*, 56C, 297–459.

Papastergiadis, N., 1998, The 'island feeling' in a changing world. In N. Papastergiadis, *Dialogues in the diasporas: essays and conversations on cultural identity*. London. River Orams Press. 215–224.

Patton, M., 1996, *Islands in time: island sociogeography and Mediterranean prehistory*. London. Routledge.

Raban, J., 2000, *Passage to Juneau*. London. Picador.

Richards, C., 1996, Henges and water: towards an elemental understanding of monumentality and landscape in late Neolithic Britain. *Journal of Material Culture*, 1, 313–336.

Robb, J., 2001, Island identities: ritual, travel and the creation of difference in Neolithic Malta. *European Journal of Archaeology*, 4.2, 175–202.

Sheridan, A., 1995, Irish Neolithic pottery: the story in 1995. In I. A. Kinnes and G. Varndell (eds), '*Unbaked urns of rudely shape*': essays on British and Irish pottery for Ian Longworth (Oxbow Monograph 55). Oxford. Oxbow. 3–21.

Sheridan, A., 2000, Achnacreebeag and its French connections: vive the 'Auld Alliance'. In J. C Henderson (ed.), *The prehistory and early history of Atlantic Europe* (BAR International Series 861). Oxford. British Archaeological Reports.

Simpson, D. and Ransom, R., 1992, Maceheads and the Orcadian Neolithic. In N. Sharples and A. Sheridan (eds), *Vessels for the ancestors: essays on the Neolithic of Britain and Ireland*. Edinburgh. Edinburgh University Press. 221–243.

Stillman, C., 1994, Lambay, an ancient volcanic island in Ireland. *Geology Today*, 62, 62–67.

Terrell, J. E., 1986, *Prehistory in the Pacific Islands*. Cambridge. Cambridge University Press.

Tilley, C., 1999, *Metaphor and material culture*. Oxford. Blackwell.

Waddell, J., 1991/2, The Irish Sea in prehistory. *Journal of Irish Archaeology*, 6, 29–40.

Wooding, J. M., 1996, *Communication and commerce along the western sealanes AD 400–800* (BAR International Series 654). Oxford. British Archaeological Reports.

Woodman, P. C., 2000, Getting back to basics: transitions to farming in Ireland and Britain. In T. D. Price (ed.), *Europe's first farmers*. Cambridge. Cambridge University Press. 219–259.

Woodman, P. C., McCarthy, M. and Monaghan, N., 1997, The Irish Quaternary Research Project. *Quaternary Science Reviews*, 16, 120–159.

Zilhão, J., 1993, The spread of agro-pastoral economics across Mediterranean Europe: a view from the far west. *Journal of the Mediterranean*, 6, 5–63.

Zilhão, J., 2000, From the Mesolithic to the Neolithic in the Iberian peninsula. In T. D. Price (ed.), *Europe's first farmers*. Cambridge. Cambridge University Press. 144–182.

Chapter 10

Coasts, mountains, rivers and bogs. Using the landscape to explore regionality in Neolithic Ireland

Carleton Jones

I first envisaged this paper as a very detailed study of the relationship between specific sites and very local landscape features in north Munster. Many years spent doing field work in this area had convinced me that the distributions of many Neolithic monuments could be profitably explored with an analysis that looked at those landscape features that constrained or enabled movement. These contrasting features combined to produce a landscape that encourages the development of route-ways along certain paths. A workable definition of a region emerged as an area defined by the intensity of its communication with other areas.

What soon became apparent, however, was that before I could focus on the detail of north Munster, Ireland as a whole had to be studied at a much coarser scale, if only to provide a broader context. It is with this goal in mind that this paper sets out to explore how the landscape may have influenced communication channels and thereby the development of regionality across Neolithic Ireland.

THE MODEL

In this model regions are not internally cohesive units interacting externally with other internally cohesive units. Instead, the extents of regions are defined by the intensity of communication. Regions meld into one another and overlap and are not defined by a perimeter boundary. Additionally, the degree of communication in one cultural sphere may not always be equal to the degree of communication in another. There can be several different 'types' of regions and these regions can overlap or subsume each other. 'Regions' as experienced by people might vary according to gender, social standing or some other variable.

As an example, there might be a large area within which intense communication in the ritual sphere was manifested in the archaeological record by a common burial practice. This large 'ritual region' might, however, contain within its extents several smaller 'trade regions' where exchange relationships between people are manifested in the archaeological record by the distribution of stone axes. Trade regions might also be different for people of different social standing. Someone of low status might be engaged in different exchange relationships from someone of high status. Marriage relationships between groups and subsequent residence shifts might produce regions of kinship that were different for men and women.

Acknowledging this complexity of relationships between people and the consequent complexity of regions avoids the culture-historical pitfall of defining a region as a bounded area within which a number of cultural traits were shared. In the model proposed here there can be a multitude of regions that could be contiguous but are very likely to be overlapping. Furthermore, where a culture-historical model would assert a normative view of culture where the shared cultural traits within a region reflected a shared worldview, the present model proposes that shared cultural traits reflect communication between people. This communication can proceed at a variety of different levels in society and between a variety of different individuals and thereby produce regions that may not be recognised or 'shared' by all members of society.

While many social factors could encourage the development of particular communication channels, environmental factors could also play a role. The model proposed here is that the landscape of Ireland facilitated communication between some areas and hindered communication between other areas. This is not an environmentally deterministic argument for the primacy of the landscape in determining communication channels. It is, however, an argument that landscape did play a role in the development of communication channels, and thereby regions, in prehistoric Ireland.

Specifically, the dangers of the west coast versus the sheltered character of the east coast; the presence of the drumlin belt dividing the north from the south; the east/west orientation of the eskers across the low-lying midlands and the uniqueness of the Bann-Barrow north/south axis down the east side of the island had important roles in the development of regionality in prehistoric Ireland. These landscape factors combined to ensure that north/south communication would always be more difficult than east/west communication and that any north/south communication would be much more intense along the east side of the country than along the west.

COASTS

The east coast of Ireland faces onto the relatively sheltered Irish Sea, while the west coast is open to nearly constant rough seas generated by low-pressure systems moving across the North Atlantic. Typically the lows hit the west coast of Ireland straight on, or from slightly to the south or north. The south and north coasts are less dangerous, but the east coast along the Irish Sea is generally safe, although subject to occasional strong southerly winds and swell. By far the safest stretch of the Irish coast is at the North Channel.

MOUNTAINS, RIVERS AND BOGS

In broad terms, Ireland is characterised by an extensive central lowland area surrounded by a mountainous periphery. Geological folding and faulting and subsequent erosion has resulted in a noticeable 'grain' in the topography that runs from the south-west to the north-east. This 'grain' turns almost due east/west in the south-west portion of the country. Ireland's topographic 'grain' makes the number of potential east/west communication routes more numerous than potential north/south routes. The only major north/south gaps through

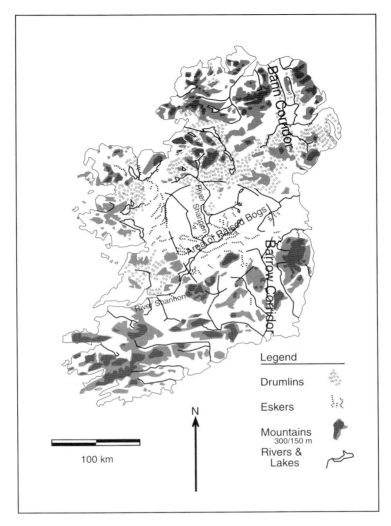

Figure 10.1 Landscape Features (after Aalen 1978 and Warren 1985).

the mountainous periphery are on the east side of the country. These are the Bann river valley in the north and the combined drainages of the rivers Slaney, Barrow and Nore in the south. As already noted, above, this pattern of mountains would mean that north/south communication was always easier in the east than in the west (Figure 10.1).

Bogs would have also acted as barriers to communication and the main area of raised bogs is located in the central lowlands (Figure 10.1). The River Shannon and its tributaries also bisect this area. The Shannon is a slow and often broad river that in places divides into numerous channels and in other places expands to form large lakes. In the winter, it floods its banks and forms 'callows', low-lying flooded areas that can stretch for great distances beyond the banks. When a bridge was built across the Shannon at Clonmacnoise in the 9th century AD it appears that in addition to the 200m bridge across the river, a lengthy gravel and clay trackway was also needed to extend the route-way across the miles of raised bogs that lie on the west bank at this point (O'Sullivan and Boland 2000). Although it is possible that the Shannon was a major transport route in prehistory, it may be that the widespread callows and bogs that stretch away from the banks in many areas reduced its utility as a routeway. It may have been too difficult to get from the actual river to dry areas beyond the callows and bogs.

Although the boggy and sometimes flooded central lowlands may have been a major barrier to communication, the area is crossed by numerous east/west trending eskers (Figure 10.1). These eskers are high ridges of well-drained gravel that form natural dry routes through the wet terrain. These include the *Eiscir Riada* that forms portions of the Early Medieval *Slighe Mhór* or 'great road' that traverses the midlands (O'Lochlainn 1940). The most significant feature of these eskers is that where they cross the central lowlands, they all run east/west, not north/south. This means that while east/west communication is facilitated across the boggy midlands, north/south communication is not aided.

Another major barrier to communication would have been the broad belt of drumlins that stretches from the east coast to the west coast on the northern edge of the central lowlands (Figure 10.1). This drumlin belt is characterised by small steep-sided hillocks (drumlins) closely packed together with lakes and bog patches filling the hollows between the drumlins (Aalen 1978). There are no convenient eskers or other straight landscape features traversing the drumlins. Routeways across the drumlin belt would have to be very twisted and tortuous as they wound around the countless watery low spots and around and over the steep-sided drumlins.

The combined effect of these landscape features is that potential east/west routeways are more common than potential north/south routeways. In addition, the contrast between the east and west coasts and the location of the Bann-Barrow corridor on the east side of the island have combined to facilitate north/south communication along the east side of the island and to hinder north/south communication along the west side of the island.

THE FIVE GREAT ROADS OF ANCIENT IRELAND

Early Medieval written sources recount the tradition that Ireland had five great roads. Although no contemporary map exists of these roads, documents list the stopping places along them (O'Lochlainn 1940; Smyth 1982). Details are open to debate (*e.g.* did the *Slighe Mhór* cross the Shannon at Athlone or further south at Clonmacnoise) and it is perhaps more accurate to view these ancient 'roads' as main channels of communication. The precise river crossing used may have been determined by the season or prevailing political situation.

It is also important to keep in mind that these 'five great roads' are merely those that the Early Medieval writers felt were the major routeways, and many lesser routes are also documented. If we assume, however, that these were the major channels of most frequent and most intense communication, an interesting pattern emerges. First, the only major route connecting the north and the south runs along the east side of the country and uses

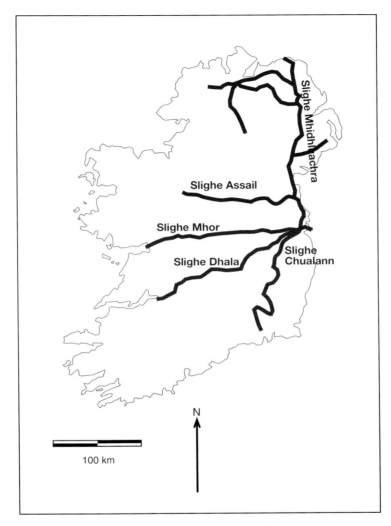

Figure 10.2 Ancient roads (after O'Lochlainn 1940).

the only major north/south gaps in the mountains that ring the island, the Bann and Barrow river valleys (Figures 10.1 and 10.2). Second, the three other major route-ways all traverse the island from east to west. The middle of these routes, the *Slighe Mhór* crosses the central lowlands and portions of the *Slighe Mhór*, follow the *Eiscir Riada*, the major east/west esker that traverses the central lowlands. To the north of the *Slighe Mhór*, the *Slighe Assail* travels from east to west along the boundary of the drumlin belt to the north and the central lowlands to the south. To the south of the *Slighe Mhór*, the *Slí Dhála* travels along the southern margin of the central lowlands (Figures 10.1 and 10.2).

The five major Early Medieval routes closely follow the constraints and opportunities offered by the landscape, as outlined above. This arrangement means that frequent and intensive communication between the north and the south was probably concentrated along the eastern side of the island. It also means that the western regions were probably in more frequent communication with regions to their east rather than with regions to their north or south.

How far back in time can we project these routeways? The accounts that historians have used to reconstruct these routes were written down some time in the second half of the first millennium AD. Some stories document journeys between Christian ecclesiastical sites and therefore only demonstrate the existence of the route after the arrival of Christianity in Ireland. It is known, however, that many ecclesiastical sites were established on existing routes rather than the route being established after the church. In addition, some stories probably relate to events that took place before the arrival of Christianity (*cf.* King 1998).

Although there were no major topographical changes in Ireland between the earlier prehistoric period and the Early Medieval period, other changes may have affected the course of routes. The most significant changes in the landscape would have been the expansion of the bogs and possibly the greater clearance of forests. The most significant technological change in transport would have been the introduction of wheeled vehicles and horses in the later prehistoric period. Therefore by the time these routes are documented in written sources, some landscape features had changed and transport had changed. Nevertheless, what is striking about the documented Early Medieval routes is their close correspondence to the constraints and opportunities offered by the landscape. It is at least possible that the origins of these routeways lie in prehistory.

THE NEOLITHIC

The communication corridor model proposed here is put forward within a framework of regional interaction. No implication of population diffusion as an explanatory mechanism is intended. Similar material culture in different regions is seen as the result of communication between regions. The use of similar symbols such as similarities in megalithic tomb architecture is viewed as the result of symbolic transfer and/or convergence. The greater the symbolic transfer/convergence, the more intense and/or sustained the communication between areas. Portable items such as stone axes found at a distance from their source are viewed as evidence for some form of material exchange between areas. Furthermore, the number of axes in an area is viewed as a reflection of either the intensity or the duration of exchange between areas. Pottery was often manufactured from local materials but incorporated design elements from farther afield. Pottery, therefore, is viewed as evidence of the exchange of either people or ideas between areas.

Megalithic Tombs, Stone Axes and Pottery

Although the traditional typology of Irish megalithic tombs is not very nuanced, it does reflect some real similarities and differences between megalithic tombs. As ritual monuments, the form of megalithic tombs is likely to have contained significant symbolic

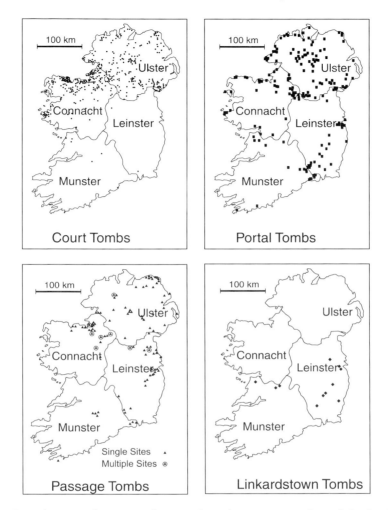

Figure 10.3 Distributions of court tombs, portal tombs, passage tombs and Linkardstown tombs (after Ó Nualláin 1989 and Raftery 1974 with additions).

elements. Similarities in architectural form, therefore, can be viewed as evidence for symbolic transfer/convergence and differences in architectural form can be viewed as evidence for a lack of symbolic transfer/convergence. Additionally, the absence of megalithic tombs in one area and their presence in another area is viewed as an absence of symbolic transfer/convergence, not an absence of people.

Both the court and portal tomb distributions show a clear north/south divide with tombs very numerous in the north and scarce in the south (Figure 10.3). This distribution could well be the related to a lack of intensive communication between these two regions. Additionally, the fact that where portal tombs do occur in the south, they are more frequent in the east than in the west may well be related to a higher degree of north/south communication along the east side of the country than along the west.

The small cluster of portal tombs in north Munster (and south Connacht) is separated by long distances from both the northern group and the south-eastern group of portal tombs. The model proposed here suggests that a communication route to the east is more likely than one going either north or south. The strongest evidence that north Munster was communicating more intensively with Leinster (the province to the east of Munster) rather than with areas to the north or to the south, comes from the distribution of Linkardstown tombs. Linkardstown tombs are absent in the north of the country but present in the two southern provinces (Figure 10.4). If the Linkardstown tomb distribution is the result of more intense communication east/west than north/south, the distribution of portal tombs in north Munster may also be the result of east/west communication with Leinster.

The distribution of passage tombs also shows a clear north/south divide with the majority of the passage tombs occurring in the north and much smaller numbers in the south (Figure 10.4). There are passage tombs in the south-east and recent discoveries have shown that passage tombs are also located in central and western Munster (Connolly 1999). Once again, however, the concentration of these southerly passage tombs along the eastern side of the country and the very large gap in the west between the Munster passage tombs and those farther north suggests more intense north/south communication in the east.

The distribution of stone axes in the Neolithic also shows a divide between north and south. Porcellanite axes, which originate in the north, are found mainly in the north while shale and mudstone axes are more frequent in the south. This distribution does not appear to be merely the result of distance from the porcellanite sources. There are regions in Britain farther from the porcellanite sources than southern Ireland where porcellanite axes are more common (Sheridan 1986; Cooney 2000). It may be that exchange contacts between northern Ireland and parts of Britain were more intense than exchange contacts between northern and southern Ireland (Figure 10.4).

Neolithic pottery in Ireland also shows evidence for regionality, with local varieties throughout the country. These regional variants are distinguished by the form of their rims, shoulders, lugs and decoration (Sheridan 1995). Interestingly though, there are also similarities in pot types that cross-cut differences in megalithic tomb architecture. Related types of decorated bipartite bowls for example have been found in northern court and portal tombs as well as in the southern Linkardstown tombs (*ibid.*).

The end of the Neolithic and the beginnings of new communication channels?

Throughout the Neolithic we can see evidence for regionality on a variety of levels. Megalithic tomb distributions reveal a pattern of symbolic transfer/convergence in some areas and differences between other areas. Stone axe distributions reveal a pattern of exchange contacts that linked some areas and excluded other areas. Pottery distributions also reveal a pattern of regionality, but one that in some cases cross-cut regions, defined by other indicators such as megalithic tombs.

This pattern of regionality was in part formed by the pattern of communication channels that were in operation. The paths of these communication channels were no doubt determined in large part by social factors, but the landscape also played a role in determining the communication channels. In this light it is interesting that patterns in the archaeological record appear to correlate with salient landscape features. Specifically, there are greater distinctions between north and south than between east and west and similarities between north and south are concentrated in the east.

At the end of the Neolithic this pattern may have changed. With the distribution of wedge tombs we have the first spread of ritual monuments suggestive of a high degree of communication on a north-south axis running up the west side of the island rather than the east (Figure 10.5). It is unclear what may have caused this shift. Perhaps an advance related to river transport (either in boat technology or perhaps in artificially constructed paths that may have aided access over the callows) opened up the potential of the River Shannon. Similarly, an advance in boat technology or perhaps even a change in weather patterns may have provided new opportunities for safe travel along the west coast. Interestingly, however, this new alignment may not have lasted. In later prehistory the old north-south distinction seems to re-emerge in various artefact distribution patterns, with one of the most notable being the almost complete restriction of beehive querns to the northern half of the island (Caulfield 1977; Waddell 1998).

What I hope this paper has provided is a model of how the large-scale landscape features of Ireland seem to have affected communication in prehistory. With this model we can

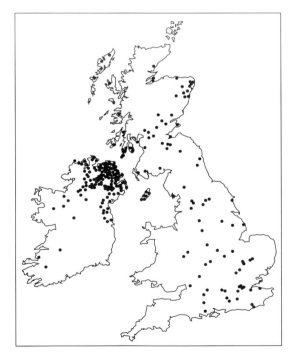

Figure 10.4 Porcellanite axe distribution (after Sheridan 1986).

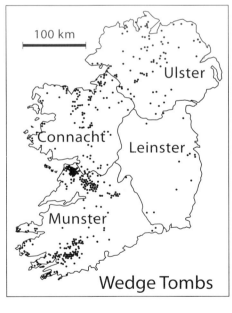

Figure 10.5 Main concentration of wedge tombs versus main concentration of Bowl Tradition pottery (after Ó Nualláin 1989 and Waddell 1992).

begin to look at the interplay between the landscape and manifestations of regionality in the archaeological record. In turn, this may help us understand the human behaviours that created the 'regions' manifested on our distribution maps.

ACKNOWLEDGEMENTS

Many thanks to Elinor Jones and Carleton Jones snr. for the speedy and skilful production of all the illustrations.

Bibliography

Aalen, F. H. A., 1978, *Man and the Landscape in Ireland*. London. Academic Press.
Caulfield, S., 1977, The Beehive Quern in Ireland. *Journal of the Royal Society of Antiquaries of Ireland* 107, 104–138.
Connolly, M., 1999, *Discovering the Neolithic in county Kerry: a passage tomb at Ballycarty*. Bray. Wordwell.
Cooney, G., 2000, *Landscapes of Neolithic Ireland*. London. Routledge.
King, H. A., (ed.) 1998, *Clonmacnoise Studies, volume 1, seminar papers 1994*. Dublin. Dúchas.
O'Lochlainn, C., 1940, Roadways in ancient Ireland. In J. Ryan (ed.), *Essays and studies presented to Professor Eoin MacNeill*. Dublin. Three Candles. 465– 474.
Ó Nualláin, S., 1989, *Survey of the Megalithic Tombs of Ireland, volume 5, Co. Sligo*. Dublin: Stationery Office.
O'Sullivan, A. and Boland, D., 2000, *The Clonmacnoise bridge: an early medieval river crossing in County Offaly*. Archaeology Ireland Heritage Guide No. 11.
Raftery, B., 1974, A Prehistoric Burial Mound at Baunogenasraid, Co. Carlow. *Proceedings of the Royal Irish Academy*, 74(10), 277–312.
Sheridan, A., 1986, Porcellanite artefacts: a new survey. *Ulster Journal of Archaeology*, 49, 19–32.
Sheridan, A., 1995, Irish Neolithic pottery, the story in 1995. In I. Kinnes and G. Varndell (eds), *Unbaked Urns of Rudely Shape* (= Oxbow Monograph 35). Oxford. Oxbow. 3–21.
Smyth, A., 1982, *Celtic Leinster, Towards an historical geography of early Irish civilization A.D. 500–1600*. Dublin. Irish Academic Press.
Waddell, J., 1998, *The prehistoric archaeology of Ireland*. Galway. Galway University Press.
Warren, W., 1985, Stratigraphy. In K. Edwards and W. Warren (eds), *The Quaternary History of Ireland*. London: Academic Press. 39–65.